THE OAK TREE THAT GREW ON A ROCK

The Life Story and Ministry of Prophet Gerbole

From the original Amharic edition
by

DEREJE BEKELE

Translated into English by Tilahun Beyene Kidane

Edited by Nathan B. Hege.

The Oak Tree That Grew on a Rock: the life story and ministry of Prophet Gerbole Hirpa. Translated into English by Tilahun Beyene Kidane.

1, Gerbole Hirpa,1962–. 2. Christian movement in western Ethiopia. 3. Biography. 4.Miracles. 5. Evangelicals. 6. Church growth.

WestBow Press books may be ordered through booksellers or by contacting:

WestBow Press
A Division of Thomas Nelson & Zondervan
1663 Liberty Drive
Bloomington, IN 47403
www.westbowpress.com
1 (866) 928-1240

ISBN: 978-1-4908-7779-2 (sc)
ISBN: 978-1-4908-7781-5 (hc)
ISBN: 978-1-4908-7780-8 (e)

Library of Congress Control Number: 2015906431

Print information available on the last page.

WestBow Press rev. date: 07/17/2015

Contents

To those heroes of the gospel, from Estifanos of Debre Berhan to Estifanos of the Ogaden and other Ethiopians of all ages who paid a heavy price—sometimes with their lives—for the sake of the gospel of Jesus Christ

Gratitude

In addition to the Lord who brought me into existence and revealed His glory through an ordinary person like me, there are many persons to whom I am indebted. First, there are those who stood with me in everything, beginning from my childhood days and the years of my persecution. Then there is my dear wife, Adanech Tolera, who, through lots of ups and downs during the years of immense difficulty, bore the burdens of the family singlehandedly—raising the children, hosting guests, supporting me—so that I could go about my ministry without a heavy heart. She often said, "Do not worry about us but go in peace and serve." She could be a model for the wives of ministers.

Next is the author of the Amharic book, Dereje Bekele, and his wife, Tadelech Degefu. I also extend my gratitude to Dr. Negussie Teferra, Pastor Bekele Wolde Kidan, and Pastor Tsadiku Abdo, who reviewed the Amharic manuscript and gave valuable suggestions. I want to thank all those who shared their knowledge about my life, both in writing and by telephone. Even if some of their viewpoints have not been included in the book because of their similarity or lack of space, their contributions will not be forgotten. Finally, I express my deep appreciation to Tiddenek Tariku for the cover design and for preparing the manuscript.

—Gerbole Hirpa

About the Second Edition

The second edition of this book was first published in Amharic in Addis Ababa, Ethiopia, in 2011. After the book took shape and came off the press, we did not expected that it would travel far. Our hope was that it would serve as a cool breeze to those who are yearning to see the glory of God and who hunger for righteousness and holiness. But as the days rolled on, the reports we received indicated that it got into the hands of many rather swiftly and reached many places around the globe. Many calls came from Europe, the United States, and Australia, informing us of its arrival and thanking us for it. We received all the appreciation and admiration cascading from various directions—each time bowing before the Lord and transferring all the honor to Him.

This book is about the forty-year walk of Gerbole Hirpa, an evangelist and minister of the gospel in Ethiopia. After the first edition, we realized that many from near and far, the educated as well as the uneducated, were being blessed by it. Furthermore, when we saw the faith of many being renewed and some receiving immediate results by calling on "the God of Gerbole," we were convinced that it should also be translated locally into Oromifa and internationally into English, so that it would be a blessing to many. Hence, the corrected and improved second edition.

—Dereje Bekele

INTRODUCTION

Stories are usually not recorded in Ethiopia because it is not a common practice. People and circumstances come and go, and we do not look back to gather lessons from the footprints they have left behind. They complete their lifecycles and pass on before we examine them up close. And when and if we want to catch up with them, we may get there just as they are interred and the eulogy is read, singing their praises. We hear the story of the person's goodness that we kept hidden in our hearts, now told in his absence. We talk about his race in life after it is all over, but we did not utter it while he was living. At the last hour, we say this and that and part ways. As time passes, the story fades from memory.

But the Bible is the written history and record of what God did with and through people. The book of Genesis, one section of the Bible, includes the story of Abraham, his children, and the people of Israel. What is more, it is the deep mystery of how God works.

By the same token, Prophet Gerbole's life and ministry is the story of the wonderful living work of God through him. We actually cannot separate one from the other and because of that, instead of reading his story after we say good-bye to him at the end of life, I have tried to write what God has done, from his childhood to gray hair, noting his faithful response to the Lord. I have tried to balance the fact that God is near and working among us today with the need for faithfulness on our part in order for Him to work through us.

Finally, important lessons have come from the life of this person who lived the past thirty-seven years in the presence of God, talking to God as well as hearing His voice. This has relevance in particular to those ministers who are anointed by God to serve the church in various ways. From time to time, we observe ministers using their anointing for their own benefit and who become agents for others seeking earthly benefits. This is sin. As often is the case, a person anointed for a small neighborhood assembly slowly expands his territory by his own efforts and tries to traverse beyond God's will. This he does to build himself up and prosper his life.

In Exodus 30:32, the commandment regarding the anointing is, "Do not pour it on men's bodies," warning us not to add moisture and beauty to our bodies. I have no doubt that the carefulness and precaution of Gerbole will serve as a warning to those who simply put their gifts on the market. Those of you who have poured the anointing on your skin and have only beautified yourselves, I entreat you to learn from this man who throughout his life never has seen receiving but always giving. Your reward will be from the Lord.

In conclusion, I would like to encourage all, including churches, to strengthen the tradition of writing the stories of persons who God uses. Such stories are part of the record of the work of God, in addition to being resources for the next generation.

Dereje Bekele, author

Foreword

Gerbole Hirpa Walks with God.

Once or twice in a generation, a man or woman appears with such childlike, profound union with God that through his or her testimony, we fall on our faces once again, like the people of Israel at Carmel, crying, "The Lord, He is God! The Lord, He is God!" There is little more that we can utter, only a life to throw in surrender at the feet of Jesus, thirsting for more of God.

Such a one is Gerbole, the Ethiopian.

True, many of us know and love God, walking with Him daily. Our lives have been forever changed. Yet not many of us have walked that path of obedient, living faith so simply, deeply, and persistently as he.

To those who long to be renewed in communion with a miracle-working God, Gerbole points the way. Even the *doqma* tree bows down to yield its fruit to the hungry child!

To those who doubt that God still provides in a materialistic age, read how Gerbole distributes eucalyptus leaves to his needy children at family altar, telling them that money is on the way. Even before they end their prayer of gratitude with nothing but eucalyptus before them, two strangers appear at the door with a gift—all they need and more.

To those who are persecuted for righteousness sake, rejoice in the story of one who even as a child was driven from his home and suffered for years as he traveled from place to place, yet was never forsaken by his heavenly Father.

To those who fearfully clutch their possessions, walk with a man who not once but year after year, throughout his lifetime, gives away all that he has at the word of God—yet receives back again and again for his own needs and those of others.

To those who believe it is a mark of sainthood and great spiritual maturity to receive revelation from God, marvel at the stranger who came day after day to a poor shepherd boy, known to him only as "I-Love-You," and led him to the truth. The stranger was Jesus, the shepherd boy Gerbole.

To those who are driven to minister to others, be challenged by the life of one who has brought healing and hope to thousands through the outflow of moment-by-moment communion with God in ordinary life—praying, giving, loving, and working at the most menial tasks, all the while witnessing miracles of healing, provision, and deliverance.

Read this book once, and you will want to read it again and again. Read it aloud with your friends, your spouse, and your children and grandchildren. Give it to the hungry, cynical, or desperate.

It is no accident, I think, that it comes from one of the poorest countries in the world and from the rural areas of that country. Remember Bethlehem. For sure, "God has chosen the weak things of the world to put to shame the things which are mighty" (1 Cor. 1:27). Gerbole was—and insists on remaining—a nobody. As a result, the glory of God shines brighter still.

Neither is it a coincidence that it comes from the heart of the "global South," where the life-giving power of the Holy Spirit has been poured out so abundantly in our time. Today, the great driving center of the Christian Church lies in Africa, Asia, and Latin America.

Perhaps it is also no happenstance that Ethiopia is the land of one of the very oldest churches in the world. God seems to take special joy in building on and renewing ancient spiritual foundations. Here he has done it once again.

May this testimony be used by the Spirit to bring joy and courage to the people of the jaded West. May new shepherd boys and girls—and prophets—like Gerbole rise up in every nation to walk with God in self-giving love.

Thank you, God, for raising up Gerbole in this generation. Thank you, Gerbole, for saying yes.

—Richard Showalter,
President Emeritus and Global Coach
The International Missions Association (IMA)
August 2014

Preface to the English Edition

This book is about a marvelous story of the Lord's sovereign selection, guidance, and faithfulness, made real in the life of a regular person. By coincidence I was able to lay my hands on a copy of the Amharic edition of *The Oak Tree That Grew on a Rock* when a friend of mine encouraged our fellowship group to take turns reading the book. He spoke so highly of it, at times bordering on high excitement, that I decided to read it—and read it quickly—to see what was in it.

I found the contents very exciting and surreal. The question that sprang up in my mind: could such things happen today in the twenty-first century? And are there modern-day Elijahs and Elishas who live in real-time relationships with the Lord and in total obedience? My next thought was about how one could go about translating it into English, so the story could reach the wider world. Not only was the language and style of writing different, but some of the stories seemed to defy common sense or logic, as understood in the Western world. At any rate, I dismissed that thought, believing that the burden would eventually fall in the lap of the person who got the job of translating the book.

One fine day in January 2012, I received a call from Asrat Alemu, a family friend whom I have known for a long time. I was not surprised by the call, because Asrat and I call each other from time to time, especially when there are occasions like birthdays and other celebrations that create an opportunity to get together. But that day, Asrat's call had a very different reason. After the initial exchange of greetings, he went straight to the purpose of the call. He asked me if I had seen the book about the prophet Gerbole and if I'd had a chance to read it, to which I replied affirmatively. He then went on to tell me that he had a very strong urge to have the book translated into English and amazingly, another brother from his church had the same intense feeling about the need to have the book translated. He told me how the two linked up and decided to take concrete steps to start the translation work.

They first had to search for Prophet Gerbole's contact information and secure his permission to start the project. In their phone conversation, Gerbole told them that eleven others had offered to translate the book and that they were number twelve. He said to them that God had affirmed to him that they were the ones to do the job. Asrat and his friend were happy and excited to get that blessing and quickly went about looking for a translator. They soon located a potential translator through a person they knew. However, there were two issues about that particular would-be translator; namely, the fact that the person was not a believer and that the price he quoted was way beyond their range.

At that point, Asrat had a dream in which he saw himself giving me the book. When he woke up, he said to himself, "Why didn't I think of Gash (Elder) Tilahun in the first place?" He took the dream as a confirmation from God, so he called me.

My answer to Asrat was that I would try to get in touch with Prophet Gerbole himself during my trip to Ethiopia, as I was preparing to go there. Although I did check with a church leader who knew Gerbole, circumstances did not allow me to meet him in person or talk to him by phone. I thought that was the end of it, as I did not expect Asrat to call me again about the translation work. But he did call back in early April 2012 to follow up on the project and in fact, he proposed to meet with me, along with his friend who was also interested in the translation of the book.

We set a date and met at our home in Columbia, Maryland, at which time we were also able to connect with Prophet Gerbole by phone. Sure enough, we were able to hear directly from him that the project was approved and blessed by the Lord. He asked me personally to call him separately at another time.

When I called him back another day, he said God told him that I was the person set aside for this job. He told me that I was not supposed to live but that God extended my life because of His love for me.

I knew then that this truly was a man of God, because it was true that I was, at one time, very, very close to death and came back literally from the brink as a result of the intense prayer of brothers and sisters. We had a very long conversation on the phone, and he blessed me and promised to stand behind me in prayer with his right hand raised.

After that phone conversation with Prophet Gerbole, I did not have any doubt that this project was ordained by God, as there was no way that human ingenuity and planning could orchestrate all this and join together Gerbole and Asrat, along with his friend and Tilahun to embark on this translation project. It was a God thing.

I embarked on the challenging and tedious translation work on April 25, 2012, dividing my time between this and other responsibilities. Like all other writing projects, there was no constant speed that I could maintain, as the work called for inspiration, which ebbs and flows. Inspiration aside, I could not even make significant progress in the spring and summer of 2012 due to prior commitments. However, my goal was to get to the halfway mark by early September but fell slightly short of my target, due to a conference trip to Ethiopia for which I was the coordinator. On that visit, my wife, Hiewet, and I were able to meet in person Prophet Gerbole and his wife, Adanech, along with the author of the Amharic version, Dereje Bekele. It was also a joy to meet the two younger children still living with them.

The project moved forward at a faster speed, beginning from October, and the rough draft was completed on December 19, 2012. After that, the manuscript went through a lot of editorial phases that helped to further refine the translation and the flow.

As one goes through the book, some questions are bound to arise in the mind of the reader. These questions may include the following:

> Is this a real story or some kind of fairy tale?
> If true, is this person in the story a normal human being?
> How is it that the story was kept hidden for thirty-seven years? And why is it being told now?
> How is it that this man of God has been able to avoid the pitfalls of money, power, and fame, living a humble life with total obedience to God?

We highly recommend that you read the book, which contains the testimonies of people who know him up close and have ministered with him. You could also do your own independent investigation. I doubt you would find any holes in the story. As mentioned above, my wife and I had the privilege of meeting Gerbole and his family (his wife and two young children) in the summer of 2012. We found them to be regular people, living in their community like all others. The one distinguishing mark we noted during our brief visit with them was that they were very loving people with radiant faces and a joyful spirit. We also had the opportunity to talk to other people who know Gerbole closely. They say the book does not contain even half of what the Lord has done in the life of this brother.

Finally, I had the opportunity to meet with Prophet Gerbole at the International Missions Association (IMA) gathered in Singapore from August 26 to September 3, 2013. There, we shared a room and came to know each other up close. He is a joyful and humble servant of the Lord with deep love for God and people. When he was not at the conference hall or meeting with people, he was on his knees or studying the Scriptures and meditating. His hours of sleep were very limited. During his stay in Singapore, he was a real blessing to the assembly, as well as to individuals.

What we learn from the life of Prophet Gerbole is obedience, obedience, and again obedience to the Lord by completely dying to self. Some believe that those who love and follow the Lord are spared from difficulties in life. However, as we note in the life of this servant of God, even persons like him pass through the valley of difficulties and hardship, because it is God's school for teaching humility and obedience that prepares us for a life of victory.

Joseph had to pass through prison before becoming the prime minister of a superpower of his era. Similarly, David had to tend sheep before being elevated to the position of a famous monarch and the ancestor of Jesus Christ himself. Jeremiah lived a life of weeping and was thrown into a pit. Jesus lived a life full of pressures and difficulties and died a horrible death. The apostles spread the good news of the gospel through extreme persecution and hardship, and all but one finally paid the ultimate price for their faith.

We have done all we could to make this English version of *The Oak Tree That Grew on a Rock* close to the original in Amharic, but there is no doubt that some of the meaning and flavor is lost in translation. There simply is no way to carry the cultural undertones and nuances to the English reader. But it is hoped that the story will flow along smoothly and that the main messages will come through loud and clear.

Gerbole grew up during the rule of the Communist regime (1975–91), led by military officers, which is best known as the *Derg*. It was a time of turmoil and chaos, with lots of persecution, suffering, and bloodshed everywhere within the borders of the nation. Therefore, the situation has had a big impact on the church and on Gerbole himself. He was born and raised in Wollega, western Ethiopia, and began his ministry there. Although he still has a wide ministry in his region of birth, the Lord has opened a wide door for him to serve the large community of Ethiopians living overseas.

First and foremost, I would like to give gratitude to the Lord, who orchestrated this translation work and opened up the possibility for the story to travel to the far corners of the globe. Only the Lord could do that, and I pray that all those who get the chance to read this book will draw closer to Him.

Second, the team expresses its love and appreciation to Prophet Gerbole and author Dereje Bekele for approving and blessing the translation project, giving the requisite permission, and standing behind us in prayer during the course of the work. On my part, I would like to note my deep appreciation to Asrat Alemu and his friend for initiating the project and giving the necessary support from start to finish. The full backing of Pastor Hanfere Aligaz was with the team from the beginning to the end, and on behalf of the team, I would like to express deep gratitude for the moral and material support.

Third, Mr. Nathan Hege and his wife, Mrs. Arlene Hege, spent many hours editing and re-editing the manuscript until it reached its final form. I am sure their joy comes from seeing the story travel to the far corners of the world, drawing people to God to walk in total obedience to Him.

Fourth, we thank Dr. Don Jacobs, Dr. David Shenk, Dr. Richard Showalter, and Dr. Conrad Kanagy for taking the time from their busy schedules to review the manuscript and give extremely valuable comments, suggestions, and encouragement.

I would also like to recognize the contributions of my wife, Hiewet Tsegay, who has been at my side from the beginning of the project, all the way through. In fact, she was so deeply involved that the team gave her the title of "manager." Aside from the support she provided to me day by day, I still remember the beautiful gift—a burgundy shirt—she surprised me with the day I finished the first draft. No wonder God created a helper for Adam.

The list of people who directly or indirectly contributed to the completion of this project is not limited to those I mentioned alone. This list is short, but I am certain that God's list contains everybody, and His recognition is superior to mine and also has eternal value.

After everything is said and done, the greatest honor and glory belongs to our Lord Jesus Christ, the real author of our lives and this story. He, by His infinite wisdom and power, orchestrated the entire thing long, long before we appeared on the scene. May the telling of this story lift up the name of Jesus all over the world and draw many into His eternal kingdom.

So the story is not about anybody, not even our dear brother Gerbole, but about the powerful ways in which God manifests Himself when we are attuned to His voice round the clock and walk in complete obedience. Such a close walk with God gives us a glimpse into the life of Adam and Eve before the fall and a foretaste of heaven for those whose names are written in the Book of Life.

For those who have a personal relationship with the Lord Jesus Christ as Lord and Savior, may this story help you to recalibrate your life so that your daily walk with Him will be in complete obedience. For those readers who may not have had a personal encounter with Jesus Christ, the Redeemer, may this book draw you to Him, who offered His life as sacrifice to save us all, and is ready to walk with us every day as a dear friend in all circumstances, and has prepared a beautiful place for us to live with Him forever.

To God be the glory! Amen!

Tilahun Beyene Kidane, Translator

CHAPTER 1

God Came Down at Horo Gudru

More often than not, action-oriented people whose lives have been transformed exhibit better results in effectively serving God and fulfilling their commitments than laid-back people. For example, the apostle Paul, as a persecutor of the church, was determined to go anywhere at his own expense to destroy the followers of Jesus. He only needed a letter of authority. Without even being sent by the Roman government or the Jewish clergy, just by his own initiative and providing his own transportation, provisions, and escort, he hurried toward Damascus.

In the same manner, he went to faraway places with the message of the gospel at his own expense. We find many people like this, who had been working hard to achieve their own personal goals but shifted their energy toward lofty goals when they came to the Lord. Mr. Roro Wata, a forerunner to the prophet Gerbole, is counted among such people.

The young Roro Wata could not tolerate the way the crown administration was oppressing the poor farmers in his own native province of Gojam in northwest Ethiopia. Roro realized the seriousness of the lack of schools for the children of the farmers and no medical services to speak of. This misery of the people burdened him. He said to himself that if he were to commit his life to a lofty goal, that goal must be to free these people from oppression. As a result, he rebelled against the government and went to the jungle. Linking up with other fighters in the jungle, in 1949 and 1950 they liberated two districts from the emperor's rule and administered them for two years. But at a time when things were going well for him and his group, he returned home, through the intervention of God, who determines the path of people, and began to live with his family. He married and started a peaceful life; then he crossed over the Blue Nile River from Gojam to Wollega Province and became a successful farmer and a prominent person.

In December 1967, Roro Wata had a dream in which he saw fireballs the size of big rocks falling down, igniting the trees and grass. In his dream, he ran to the river to prevent the fire from falling on him and burning him. He thought that if the fire fell on him, he would dunk in the water and save himself. However, the fire fell on him before he was able to jump in the water. Strangely, he liked it, because it was a different type of fire from any fire he knew.

Around that time, Roro took his sick son, who had visited various witch doctors in search of a cure, to the place where Mr. Mekuria Mulugeta, a schoolteacher by profession, and his group were praying. There, his son was healed. Roro repented of his sins and came to faith in the Lord.

This person who was fighting for the oppressed clung to the true liberator when he found Him. He became strong in the ministry of prayer and fasting and preached the gospel, even crossing the Nile River, going all the way to Gojam, his birth province. Using shortcuts and trails with which he was familiar, he crossed the rough terrain. Because God was with him, his ministry was accompanied by wonders and miracles. And just as he had seen in his dream, huge balls of fire, initiating mighty works of God, came down from heaven. In order to be a hard-working servant of this fire, Roro untied his oxen, hung up his plow, and became a full-time minister.

When he ministered in Gojam, those who heard his amazing story followed him back to Wollega. Fifty to sixty people, seeking to be healed of various ailments, swam across the Blue Nile River, searching for the man who, in those days, went around with a book in his hand. Not only did Roro pray for the healing of individuals but also for whole villages affected by typhoid epidemics; he was much sought after as a healer. In this way, he chased death from various localities.

Slowly, his fame spread, and Roro became a sought-after problem solver and messenger of God, even in faraway places. One time, when a typhoid epidemic was spreading and mowing down people, he received the message: "Please hurry and come to us." When the messengers arrived, he was actually plowing his field. He quickly unhitched the oxen from the plow and yoke and ordered his children to take them home. He then washed and changed clothing, took his Bible, and was on his way.

After many hours of walking, Roro arrived at the village affected by the typhoid epidemic. Generally, when an area is affected by typhoid, many get sick, and other people dare not come close to care for them. No one would stop by to even fetch water for them from the river or *isat lemechar* (bring hot coals from a neighbor to light a fire).

The dead are buried by close relatives, who have the obligation, or those who have the milder form of the disease, or by survivors. This kind of burial was not the proper type but done just to put the body in the ground.

Gerbole still remembers when his family was affected by typhoid:

> Our parents and five of the children got sick. I got better quickly because I had been exposed to it earlier, and I became the only healthy person to take care of six patients. One of the symptoms of the disease is very high fever; hence, it causes hallucinations and babbling. The community avoided us altogether. Later, our aunt, who put herself at great risk, came and baked bread for us, but at the end of the day, she went home without staying overnight. Therefore, it became my job to take care of all other chores, such as handling the cattle, fetching water from the river, going to the market, and buying provisions like coffee and salt. When I went out to run errands, I had to close the door on my sick family and leave them alone to themselves.
>
> Each time I returned from my errands, my joy knew no limits when I found all of them alive. What used to sadden me was when I found them burning with extreme thirst because they could

> not get up and help themselves. They were forced to wait for me. And I could not return quickly because of all I had to take care of.
>
> For one thing, the Welkesa River, where I fetched water, and Ticho market are not close by. Even my mother, who gave birth to ten children, used to get up from her bed on the third day to cook for the family. With typhoid, she could neither help herself nor her children. My hardworking father, who never entrusted his cattle and farm to anyone and who was a premier farmer, was at that point defeated. I served as the lone "doctor and nurse" not knowing the difference between day and night. Finally, all recovered, one by one, without anyone being lost.
>
> Oh! If only there had been someone who had a solution, and we could have sent for help!

It was to this environment, filled with misery and where many people fell like leaves, that Father Roro was called. As soon as he reached the area, he requested a hut where he could spend time in prayer. As soon as the place was readied, he began a three-day prayer and fasting regimen. He declared spiritual war on the spirit of death through his prayer. When he understood that the Lord had given him victory, he opened the hut and came out.

He picked one from among the multitude of sick people, propped him up, and commanded the disease by saying, "You widely entrenched disease and death, I command you in the name of Jesus Christ to leave this area as this sick person stands here representing all the sick people." And truly, that person, as well as the others, got healed, and the region was cleansed of typhoid.

Over time, Roro did extensive work to spread the message of the gospel by linking up with ministers who, at the time, were coming from Addis Ababa, one of whom was Dr. Haile Wolde Michael, a traveling minister and an evangelist. One time when Haile was put in jail for preaching the gospel, Roro had him released by being his guarantor, and they ministered together.

Roro tells the story of their being surrounded by a large pack of hungry and angry hyenas; they knew they could be attacked. This happened in the middle of the night at a location where they were sleeping under a tree. Roro said that the hyenas dispersed when Dr. Haile called the name of the Lord.

Another time, when we were traveling through the forest during the hot and dry season, a wildfire started, trapping them on all sides. When both called the name of the Lord, the flames died down and turned to smoke, through which they were able to escape.

All those who came to faith at that time used to do big miracles in the name of the Lord. For instance, there was a lady called Zeritu who was famous because of her beauty and wealth. She believed in the Lord Jesus Christ at a time when she was still famous and had the important people and officials of the community in the palm of her hand. She started to witness about the Lord to all those who were captivated by her beauty, and the Spirit of the Lord was working through her. Demons were cast out and the sick were healed. Her business flourished.

These were the things that ignited the fire, the embers of which reached Ebentu, Gerbole's area. Therefore, Gerbole and his ministry are the result of that visitation from God. The manifestation of the Holy Spirit, the like of which had never been seen before in Ethiopia, began in Horo Gudru in1968 and spread to the entire region. Even though the finger of God touched all believers, in no other place did fire come down in such a big way, according to Father Roro Wata's dream. Therefore, one could say that the Holy Spirit movement in Horo Gudru was really special.

CHAPTER 2

Gerbole's Childhood Years

Horo Gudru is one of the districts of the former province of Wollega in western Ethiopia, and Ebentu is one of the subdistricts. Ende serves as the main town and as such, it had within it government offices that provided services like policing, education, justice, basic health, and administration. Horocho is one of the many localities within Ebentu.

This area, with an elevation of 4,000 to 6,000 feet, has a moderate climate. The topography is undulating and flat in some places. While the plain is farmland and grassland, in the valleys and river basins, *shola doqma,* strawberry, *agam*, *qega*, and *warka* are grown.

The major rivers are Degagule, Legedabi, and Degeafeli. Originating high in the mountains, they flow into the Blue Nile. These rivers traverse the thick forest without being exposed to the hot sun, quenching the thirst of many along the way with their clean, cool waters. Building their strength from the tributaries that join them, they create cascading waterfalls where there are cataracts and gorges. Yes, they travel and indeed, they travel far. Nourished by the blessing that comes down from the heavens during the long rainy season, stretching from the end of April to the middle of October, the earth conceives life. Life grows out of the soil and bears fruit. Wild life, such as leopard, hyena, dik-dik, monkey, baboon, colobus monkey, wild boar, and various types of birds, teem within the forest. Since there is rain for the grass, grass for the deer, and deer for the leopard, nature keeps the ecological balance by providing adequate food and agreeable habitat for all. Life is peaceful there.

Along the edges of the forest in open spaces, thatched-roof houses dot the area in clusters and pairs close to the scattered farms. In the morning and evening, the smoke that rises like pillars from the houses enables one to identify homes of individuals. Frolicking calves and lambs who cannot venture far and the cackling chickens digging for food add beauty to the homesteads. Potatoes, onions, corn, and cabbage grow in the backyard gardens. In the larger fields, *teff* (grain used to make *injera,* the pancake-like bread eaten with *wot*, or sauces and stews, at every meal), *dagussa,* peas, beans, wheat, barley, and the like are grown. In general, the surroundings are rich in everything and lack nothing, except the fact that the area is behind in modernity.

Mr. Hirpa Qote and Mrs. Terefech Begna, a couple, established themselves with their family in this community and were well known and respected. Their home is one where nine children were born, including the living and those who died in their infancy. Mother Terefech had eight pregnancies and nine children. She gave birth to twins, Gerbe and Gerbole, in 1962. The girl, Gerbe, died in infancy, while Gerbole thrived.

When he turned nine, Gerbole took responsibility to look after the sheep and followed the flock to the field. Along with this, he fetched water from the river to help his mother. He also served his father, which put him above the other children. When sent on errands, he satisfied one's heart because he was quick and delivered messages correctly. He not only delivered messages but also the heart of the sender.

Mr. Hirpa was a kind and compassionate person who helped needy people. He was an honorable man and a good farmer who led a middle-class life. He would have Gerbole take some grain right from the threshing floor to old folks and disabled people. He did this at night or early morning in secret, and Gerbole would deliver the gifts but keep the secret to himself.

In 1973, this eleven-year-old boy, while going about his routines and looking after the sheep flock, started an unending stream of questions about the existence, beginnings, and purpose of nature. He would ask himself, "Who created the mountain and river? Who makes the water cascade down the mountainside? How is it that the grass, grazed by the sheep every day, grows again?"

In this way, he would ask questions about birds of the air and their beauty, about wild animals and their situation and wonder all day. This question-filled boy did not even want to play and mingle with other shepherds. He spent the entire day and night in deep thought, trying to figure out things.

One day, a man came to him while he was alone in the field, as usual, watching the sheep. This man was handsome with long hair and walked barefoot like Gerbole himself. But his feet did not seem to have been touched by the dust and mud of the surroundings, because they looked beautiful and clean. The person came close to Gerbole and said to him, "I came to be your friend because you are alone." The boy became very happy, because he did not have a friend. He asked in an anxious way, "Will you stay with me?"

The stranger assured him, with a captivating smile, that he was a friend who would stick with him for a long time. "I love you. I will be your friend. I will not leave you," he answered.

In order to know more about his new friend, Gerbole asked basic investigative questions: "Who are you? Where did you come from?"

The stranger replied, "I will tell you who I am and where I came from another time." Thus, he postponed his response, but that handsome new friend who was clothed in a beautiful outfit and who walked with his snow-white bare feet continued to come to Gerbole. Each time he came, the boy would notice him suddenly standing at close proximity and not approaching from afar. He moved with him and sat with him. They would spend the day together and part after the sheep were put in the fold. Because he did not tell his name and repeatedly told him, "I love you," Gerbole called him by the name, I-Love-You. When the sheep wandered away he would say, "I-Love-You, please bring back the sheep." The man would drive them back to where he was. In this way, Gerbole and I-Love-You spent the day together with full understanding of each other.

When Gerbole would reach the grazing field with the flock in the morning, he would look around for I-Love-You, wondering where he might have spent the night—near the river or in a tree. When he would call out, "I-Love-You, where are you?" the man would appear instantaneously. They would spend the day together.

In fact, I-Love-You would also talk to Gerbole in his dreams at night. One night in his dream, the man asked these questions: "Who created the ants? Who made them work in a systematic and orderly way? Who made your two legs walk by turn, your two hands support each other, and your two eyes focus? Who created these riddles and gave them to you?"

In this way, the man asked Gerbole many nature-related questions, begging for answers that Gerbole wanted to know. The little boy answered, "I do not know."

"Ask your father and mother when you get up in the morning, and bring me the response"—this was the assignment given him. So Gerbole popped the questions to his father and mother while they were at the morning coffee ceremony. "Who created all these?" he asked.

They responded by saying, "God created them," and added, "But you are only a child and should not worry about such things; instead, eat your breakfast and take the flock out to the field." In this way, his parents introduced him to God, just as Eli did to Samuel, and helped him to understand in a straight and unified way that God is the Creator of the world and every creature in it.

> Now Samuel did not yet know the Lord; The word of the Lord had not yet been revealed to him. The Lord called Samuel a third time, and Samuel got up and went to Eli and said, "Here I am; you called me." Then Eli realized that the Lord was calling the boy. So Eli told Samuel, "Go and lie down, and if he calls you, say, 'Speak, Lord, for your servant is listening'. "So Samuel

> went and lay down in his place. The Lord came and stood there, calling as at the other times, "Samuel, Samuel!" Then Samuel said, "Speak, for your servant is listening." (1 Samuel 3:7–10)

The following day, I-Love-You raised the issue about creation and the assignment he had given Gerbole. "Who did they tell you created these things?"

Gerbole answered, "They told me it is God who created them."

I-Love-You confirmed to him that it was correct, that God was the one who created all things. "For who is God besides the Lord? And who is the rock except our God?" (Psalm 18:31).

Gerbole remembers clearly the time he came to know God: "I loved God and in my ears, I used to hear a voice calling the name of God repeatedly." The boy who met God in person shares his memory with us: "I found the person I loved and God as one and the same in my heart."

In this way, the friend, whose identity Gerbole now understood, spent one year teaching and counseling him in the field, by the side of the river, and at his house, by day and by night. While this boy was talking with his "beloved," he was the only one who could see and hear the voice; onlookers heard only Gerbole's voice. As a result, people started saying, "Gerbole is talking to himself." So both his family and the community started to believe that Gerbole no longer was normal.

The second assumption was that if he was not talking to himself, the only possibility was that he was talking to a spirit. The parents, who were highly troubled by the situation, could not just let it go after talking about it to other people. They needed to find out with whom their son was talking, and for that, they assigned their trusted older son to investigate. His job was to go to the field with Gerbole and, in a round-about way, find out to whom the boy was talking.

The investigator spent the whole day doing his assignment with full alertness. But the younger brother continued to talk with the invisible partner. The older boy searched near and far, just in case someone was hiding in the bush, but could not find anything. Therefore, when he returned home in the evening, he gave a brief and clear report: "I did not see anything. He talks only to himself."

After the report about Gerbole talking to himself became public, the family reached the conclusion that their son was sick. As a result, they watched and cared for him so that he would not fall and hurt himself. They made sure that he was not sent far away and that he did not go to the river alone, and when he watched the sheep, the family would keep an eye on him. When necessary, someone would stay with him as his double. He was no more seen as someone capable of moving about and functioning on his own.

Meanwhile, the news that "God has come down in Amuru town" in Horo Gudru reached Ebentu. Here is how it happened:

Toward the beginning of the 1960s, foreign missionaries started providing medical services and preaching the gospel. However, because of the language and cultural barriers between them and the people, the result was not as expected. But because God had planned to do something in the land, and the government had assigned national believers as school teachers, the gospel was preached, and prayers for the sick produced wonders and miracles.

People were delivered of evil spirits, shrieking from afar. Because the people were really oppressed by many illnesses and difficulties for a long time, word about the solution to their problems was spread from person to person.

"Land of Zebulun and land of Naphtali, the way to the sea, along the Jordan, Galilee of the Gentiles—the people living in darkness have seen a great light; on those living in the land of the shadow of death a light has dawned" (Matthew 4:15–16).

Likewise in the land of Amuru in Horo Gudru, in the land across the Blue Nile River, the people living in darkness saw a great light. The good news about this great light was that it traveled as far as Ebentu district, to Horocho locality and Gerbole's village, and to his home. After that, people prepared their provisions and traveled to Amuru, where miracles were happening. Some took their sick and infirm, and others went out of curiosity to see what was happening. Teacher Mekuria Mulugeta and his companions were there in Amuru, preaching the gospel and praying for the sick. When those in Gerbole's home heard the news, they thought they had found a solution to their problem. They sent the elder brother to fetch the medicine. When he returned after several days, he did not return with medicine to swallow or some kind of ointment, as they had expected. What he found and brought for the sick boy was a changed life and a new Bible.

What the brother encountered in Amuru was hearing the gospel and believing in what he heard, repenting, and changing his life and knowing salvation through Jesus Christ. He returned as a believer in the Lord. The first thing he did after he returned was to gather his family and say, "Let us deny Satan, believe in the Lord Jesus Christ, and destroy the altar of the Devil and stop sacrificing to the spirits, the trees, and beads." After he said this, he demolished the altar in the house and threw it outside.

In those days in that area, it was customary to have an elevated corner in each home that was used as an altar for evil spirits. Whenever they cooked food, brewed coffee, or milked the cows, they would put some food on the altar for the evil spirits before they used any for themselves. Those who went to Amuru and saw the miracles God was doing and heard the gospel returned home and dismantled their altars, as Gerbole's brother had done.

In addition, although he did not know how to read, the brother would open his new Bible and say, "Fear God; abandon Satan," and standing on just one foot, he would pray, spreading his hands heavenward. "Jesus, save me. Make me your child." In addition, he reached the people living in the area with the gospel message, testifying that Jesus saves. Gerbole also started to believe and to say, "Jesus saves," just like his brother. Even though God had already personally met Gerbole, he found knowledge of what to believe in an organized way. For a time, it was said that Gerbole's and his brother's sicknesses become one and the same.

After his brother told him about the gospel, the friend who was talking to Gerbole day and night was revealed to him as Jesus Christ. When Gerbole relates this experience today, he says that Jesus told him, "I am the One who came to save you, to suffer for you, the One who died and rose again, who has the key to death and hell, and the One who will return in glory."

Gerbole's big brother, who did not get spiritual support and nurture, could not continue, because there was no one to feed the fire that started to burn in his heart. It was extinguished after burning for just a very short time, like a matchstick. His inability to read kept him from sustaining himself for a longer period. As a result, he slowly grew cold, to the point where he abandoned even calling the name of the Lord.

As it is natural to abandon one thing when choosing another, he left the Lord and went back to his old faith. He rebuilt the altar he'd torn down in broad daylight and began his worship of evil spirits.

After this, the thing about Jesus was left to Gerbole. Actually, the main purpose of the brother's trip was to seek a solution to Gerbole's problem, and in fact, he had completed the assignment. He had brought the solution of "Jesus saves." It would have been good if he had remained saved himself, but to Gerbole's family, the previous "he is sick," plus "Jesus saves," made the situation worse, denying them peace and comfort. They decided to force Gerbole to abandon his faith, and for this, his mother was chosen to lead the process.

One day, after handing him a small bag from the Wonji sugar factory with a picture of candy and an elephant on it, his mother said to Gerbole, "Come; we are going to visit relatives." She walked ahead of him while he walked behind. Following the narrow footpath that led to the big road, they hastened forward. While they were walking, the mother said, "My son, at the place we are going, the name you usually call on is not appreciated, so you might as well stop calling that name now, so that you will not do it there."

They actually were going to Wolete, the witch doctor, not to visit relatives. After completing all the ceremonial greetings, the mother spoke about the purpose of her visit. She said, "My son is sick and does not have rest day and night. He talks to himself, and I am afraid about his future, as I do not believe he can go out of the house and come in safely. Will this child grow or die? I want to know the truth." In this way she presented her petition, crouching before the witch doctor in tears.

Wolete began her duties after coffee was roasted and the boy's palm read. She then went on to tell the mother what to try and how to do it. In great shock and tears, the mother asked, "What will happen to my son?"

To see his mother distraught and crying shocked Gerbole, and he said, "Lord Jesus, control this woman. She has scared my mother. Please control her." As soon as he uttered these words, Wolete, the witch doctor, fell down with a wild shriek. The neighborhood was disturbed by her loud cry, and everything became topsy-turvy. Because Jesus felled Wolete, Gerbole was elated and said, "Jesus, you are the man," as one would say about any capable and strong man in that area. As they started their return journey, the mother said, "My son, you embarrassed me. Didn't I tell you not to call that name at that place?"

"Mother, what could I do? It came to me, and I spoke." After that incident, the mother did not take him to a witch doctor again.

Nevertheless, the solution that Wolete had whispered to Gerbole's mother in secret had to be tried—and that was to take a black chicken and a knife to the river very early in the morning, before the birds started to sing and people began to cross it or draw water from it; then kill the chicken at the waterfall, throw it away, and head back home the same way, without looking back. To implement this, the mother bought the chicken and woke up early in the morning to instruct her daughter about what was to be done. She awakened Gerbole and sent them off, saying, "My son, do as your sister tells you, and I will buy you nice boots and clothing and anything you want." Gerbole carried the chicken and the knife and went to the river with his sister.

After showing him the appropriate place, his sister gave the instructions to him, in fear and shaking. "Okay, now kill the chicken quickly, and throw it away over there. Then turn around and follow me." The boy did not move quickly, as expected, so his sister shouted angrily, "Quick—cut off its head and throw it away!"

Because cutting the head off and throwing the chicken down the precipice did not make sense to Gerbole, he said to his sister, "There must be someone to receive it from me. Who do I give it to? Where is the one receiving the chicken?"

"Kill the chicken, throw it away, and follow me," she repeated angrily. He cut off the head of the chicken. When she heard the chicken fluttering and shaking, she said, "Enough! Now, follow me," and she started to walk. Because the instructions were not to look back, both of them walked briskly, single file, like a horse and cart, and reached their homestead.

Their family who hoped that the boy would be healed met them as a group. The mother made a loud cry, fell on the ground and rolled. She then said, breaking fresh grass and tossing it in the air, "We have transgressed (*abeskugeberku*), rescue us; forgive us. In as much as he bears his own burden, you exact the dues from him."

In actual fact, Gerbole had not thrown away the chicken as he was supposed to do. Instead, he had carried back the dead chicken on his shoulder, with his clothes covered by blood, and reported that there was no one to receive it from him. In addition to bringing back the sacrifice, he had whetted the appetite of Satan and not given him his due. The family felt the reprisal would be on them. So their strong supplication was, "We are your servants. You exact it from the person who has rebelled against you." To his sister, they said, "You come in," but Gerbole, who was shivering and standing alone, was told not to mix with other people. "Go and throw away the chicken and your clothes into the valley," they told him.

It was after this that the heart of Mrs. Terefech, his mother, was broken by sorrow and hopelessness. She was sure he would die, because she knew very well that Satan does kill, and she did not understand that God is able to save. Gerbole's work assignments were reduced, believing that he did not have much time left to live. To make him feel happy, they gave him new clothes and a pair of boots from the shipment that had just arrived in their own store. The boy felt comfortable, with peace on the inside and new things on the outside, but people did not recognize his happiness.

His father, however, who traveled to the market every Saturday as a trader of salt, would say to him, "My son, since your omen is good, hand me my cane, so that I will be successful." And he would return, having achieved success. His mother, on her part, would say, "Hand me my umbrella, so that my business will go well." They would also bring a sick person to their home and say to Gerbole, "Please touch him." And when he would touch him, the person would be healed. People who had sick cattle, a cow that refused to be milked, or an ox that had become stubborn when being yoked would have Gerbole touch the animal, and the situation would change.

Mr. Hirpa had a special love for this boy, his son and confidant. Before Mr. Hirpa's death, he called Gerbole to his bed and asked him to bring salt. Gerbole brought a block of salt from the supply kept for the market. "Lick it," the father said. Gerbole licked it. His father blessed him, saying, "May you be tasty like this salt. May you be used to make things taste better, my son."

CHAPTER 3

KNOWING THE LORD

After the young Gerbole killed the chicken on the bank of the river and carried it home on his shoulder, it dawned on him that something was happening to his health. He felt sick. There was a heavy burden on his shoulders, weighing him down. Although it was not visible to other people, it was real to him. To him, it felt like a sack full of sand that would not come off his shoulders. The proof for this is that his shoulders were sore from the load he was carrying; he got tired because of the load. Because of his tiredness, he could not breathe freely. His strength was depleted. People said he had a heart problem. He slept a lot. Finally, he was bedridden.

Gerbole's older sister, Abezu, had been married and was living at a place called Daregos. One time when she came to visit the family, she asked, "What became of that boy who does not lack for troubles?"

They said to her, "He has a heart problem." After thinking for a while, she said, "Since there is a place of prayer in our community where sick people get healed, he will be cured if he goes there; otherwise, he will die right here where he is lying."

In this way, the sister, who was not a believer, preached to the family about how one could be healed by believing. Some among the family were visibly unsettled and murmured (*gumgum alu*) about the possibility that if he went there, he might not only be healed but might also change his religion. But his mother used her veto power, saying that if he could be healed, let him follow any religion. She moved to the corner where he was lying and beckoned the men for help. "Come; carry him," she said.

The relatives and neighbors were always around, because it was thought he would die any minute. Even Abezu, who lived far away, came, because she was concerned, although she used visiting the family as an excuse. The boy's breathing slowed down sometimes, and at other times it would come back. It was difficult to tell whether he was dead or alive. Some even wished to themselves that he would die and be buried, so the situation could be over.

Three men who were ready to face the problem head-on approached where Gerbole was lying. The pile of covers on the boy was much larger than his body, because he felt very cold and was shaking at times. When they uncovered him, his body was emaciated.

Evangelist Seketa Geleta was the minister and leader of the Daregos prayer chapel. He prayed for the boy who was carried into the chapel. "The load, which was visible only to me and weighed down my shoulders, fell off," Gerbole said, when talking about the instantaneous healing he received. "Death rolled off of me. The pain and tiredness I used to feel, starting from my heart, came off me like clothing. I was filled with peace and health."

Since it was said that he should stay right there at the prayer chapel until he felt better and could stand and walk on his own, the people who brought him left. Gerbole's previous spiritual experience was limited to knowing that God is the Creator of all; he also knew the word of the gospel, that Jesus saves, which his brother brought from a distant place. Truly this is the pillar of spiritual life, but a person has to learn the detailed truth. But no one had read the Bible to Gerbole or fed him spiritual food to make the truth he had grasped grow within him.

"I planted the seed; Apollos watered it, but God made it grow" (1 Cor. 3:6).

There are a series of steps that cannot be skipped for a person to believe, to be transformed and have the gospel take root. This little boy, who was carrying within him knowledge beyond his capacity, was being tossed to and fro because he could not get the teaching that would ground him in his faith. He went to the witch doctor and then to the river and now to the prayer chapel—this last one is good. His stay at the Daregos prayer chapel was a golden opportunity that enabled him to get spiritual nurturing that he had not received. Hearing the Word of God and singing spiritual songs made Gerbole swim in spiritual blessings, like a fish taken from dry land and put back in its habitat. "That was when I decided to be like Evangelist Seketa," Gerbole said when talking about the decision to enter the ministry. He reached that point after processing and settling things within himself.

The boy who was carried to Daregos returned home fully healed, filled with spiritual food, singing, and jumping up and down. After that, he would go once in a while to that chapel to worship and have fellowship with people. "When I began to meet with the people of God, seeing the Lord in the physical stopped," he said. "After that, I was limited to hearing His voice only." This indicates that fellowship with the people of God has a very high value. It is like being with the Lord Himself, because where we gather in twos or threes, the Lord is there with us, and this enables us to grasp the truth about that hope.

Gerbole remembers the last time the Lord appeared to him in the body. "He told me, 'You will not die; you will live. I have given you the covenant treasures of faith and love, goodness (*kininet*) and humility, mercy and generosity, and patience and perseverance.' After that He put them around my neck, as one would a medallion, and said, 'All people to the ends of the earth will read these on you and benefit, and you will be the servant of these treasures. For this, I have appointed you.' Then he left. After that, He came to me through His voice and not in a physical body. My life was changed after that. I began to experience the Lord, and my faith grew deeper."

Gerbole thinks 1974 was the year he accepted the Lord. Even though he was not able to read, in 1975 he bought a Bible for fifteen cents. Because it is the Word of God, he loved it and never parted with it. He says the friend he called I-Love-You gave it to him as a replacement for Himself. Sick people got healed when Gerbole touched them with his Bible.

The matter about the healing had surprised even his mother. The matter of health has been everyone's concern since the fall of this world, so his mother said, "Please cut some plant and give it to me, so that when I touch it in the name of Gerbole's God, I will be healed." Gerbole said to her, "I will not give it to you, but if you want Jesus, the Lord of the healing, accept Him and make Him Lord of your life." But it was only after many years that she came to know the Lord.

Slowly, both the family and community began to hate him. This was in spite of the fact that he did good things, like praying for them when they got sick and running errands when they asked him.

"If the world hates you, keep in mind that it hated me first. If you belonged to the world, it would love you as its own. As it is, you do not belong to the world, but I have chosen you out of the world. That is why the world hates you. Remember the words I spoke to you: 'No servant is greater than his master. If they persecuted me, they will persecute you also. If they obeyed my teaching, they will obey yours also'" (John 15:18–20).

They evicted Gerbole from the house, saying, "You are now healed and can go anywhere you want or mix with your kind of people and live with them." At that moment, he could not think where to go. He thought of a cave that was the hideout of wild animals.

The forest of Degagule, where wild animals like wild boar and pigs lived, had a narrow entrance that led to a cave. Inside the cave was a flat rock, like a table. Gerbole would sneak inside the cave and sleep on this rock at night. Sometimes, he would just hide and live in the forest and pray. Keneni, his elder brother's wife, loved Gerbole very much and had compassion for him. She told him that she would prepare food and place it in an empty beehive among other hives, and he would go there in the dark and pick up his meals. Unless he went to the chapel in Moger or Daregos, he would get his meal at least once a day. But later, his little brother and a certain dog found out the secret and started to steal his food. There were actually three beneficiaries waiting for that food supply, and whoever got there first ate it.

CHAPTER 4

The Oak Tree That Grew on a Rock

The place where I saw oak trees on a plain is Arsi, Neghele, in south-central Ethiopia. Those trees grow on level ground and continue to get plenty of water, as their roots extend in any direction and are interwoven like a spider web. Other than that, the majority of oak trees I have seen are those that grow on and cling to the edges of gorges and cliffs. One oak seed, not knowing where it came from, fell on a rock. This little seed, not knowing its "mother" or "father" and transported by either the wind or a bird, had big courage. Even if it did not have a father and a mother, it began to germinate and grow on the rock. The conditions needed to grow, such as air, water, warm temperature, and soil, are not found on the rock. Using the leaves falling from trees, the dust blown in by the wind, and the dew in the night, this little seed germinated, sending its roots downward, and it shot upward under conditions in which growth seems impossible.

Even during the dry season, when the rock heated up like a skillet, the little oak tree somehow did not get roasted. It passed through those hot months, clinging to the rock. Meanwhile, it did not sit idle, but while clinging to the hard and strong rock, it silently did some serious work for tomorrow. It split what was easy to split and circumvented what was impossible, and in this way, the oak that grew on a rock established its residence there. It thus continued to live on the edge of the cliff, with its roots longer than its trunk. Before it was seen firmly standing as a big tree, it passed through difficult years, with its roots bleeding.

Before little Gerbole was firmly planted in Christ, the Rock, and before he became a cover and resting place for others, he went through times of testing and serious difficulties. Since his family and the community hated, ostracized, and forced him to leave the area, he left home and started his journey. "I left with just my Bible, not knowing where I was going," said Gerbole, who left home as a very young boy without any food, money, or spare clothes. Since Christians were the closest to him next to his parents, he headed toward the chapel, where Evangelist Duressa Dinsa was serving. He knew that there, he could share about the situation he faced and seek counsel.

Since the place was far, and he had been pushed out without a meal, he felt hungry and tired. After all, what could one find on the narrow road that passed through the forest, other than fatigue? As he was looking left and right for fruits on trees, he saw a *doqma* tree, loaded with its ripe fruit. He approached it. But the tree was high, and the famished boy was at a distance from the fruit, where they could not meet. For the boy, it was imperative to eat that *doqma*, regain strength, and continue his travel. He therefore needed help from the Jesus he loved to make the fruit fall from the tree. Just as soon as he uttered, "Lord Jesus, send some birds to make the fruit fall down," he heard a voice telling him to move away from under the tree. Jesus did not need to command birds that would bring down fruit with their beaks. For this obedient servant, He did not offer the leftovers from birds but rather laid a table before him. The huge *doqma* tree was commanded to bow down before Gerbole. The tree, loaded with ripe fruit, bowed down like a half moon in the direction the boy was standing. Gerbole was awestruck. His heart raced. His legs began to shake. He could not believe what had happened before his very eyes.

Gerbole knew the Lord. There were times when he saw Him with his very own eyes and spent the day and night with Him. It was at this point that he understood that Jesus would be with him for the rest of his life and that he would live a miracle-filled life. More than the tree bearing ripe fruit that bent before him, it was the closeness of the Lord that captivated him at a time when friends and relatives disowned him. Gerbole understood that this was a friend who would not abandon him, one on whom he could rely.

He said, "I felt satisfied to know how much the Lord loves me and is with me at a time when I thought I was all alone and wandering in the wilderness, so I only ate a little. Even if people hated me, the fact that God is with me made me feel full. This gave me assurance that I am not a wanderer and gave me strength and renewal more than the food."

Gerbole related his own story to that of the blind man who was healed by Jesus and thrown out by the Jews. He remembered that "Jesus heard that they had thrown him out" and that the blind man went to Him (John 9:34–35).

Even after the wandering boy ate its fruit and went his way, the *doqma* tree did not straighten up. It stayed in the same bent position; it remained bent like a bow and continued to be called Gerbole's *doqma* for a long time. Eventually, children and women chipped away at it to use it for firewood, reducing it to a stump. It stood as a testament to people who lived outside the will of God. "The God of Gerbole" and "Gerbole's *doqma*" were words uttered for a long time by young and old.

When he reached the home of Evangelist Duressa Dinsa, the believers embraced and kissed him, with all shedding tears. When he told them that he'd come because of persecution, they were happy that this happened to him because of Jesus, but they were protective and compassionate toward him, as he was only a child.

In just a few days, he forgot all that had happened to him and continued to worship and be encouraged by the believers. Wherever Evangelist Duressa went to minister, he checked if there was anyone who would take in this homeless boy. Finally, a brother called Anbessa Aga was willing to give him shelter. The area was at a higher altitude and mostly covered by forest. The evangelist Duressa took him there and handed over the responsibility for the boy to serve and live in that brother's house.

At the home of Anbessa Aga, Gerbole's job was to watch and protect the crops in the fields from wild animals. When returning home in the evening, he was to collect firewood and carry it home. He also fetched drinking water from the river, carrying the container on his shoulder.

In the evening, he washed people's feet. After all this, he did not eat his supper and go to bed, like others. Since the believers of that area used a little house as a place of prayer, he went there and spent the night in prayer. And in the morning, he would do what he had done the previous day. Thus, his cycle of activities and routines would continue. When he met people, he would testify about salvation in the Lord. He told them that he was persecuted because of his faith in the Lord and testified to them that they too should believe and be prepared to pay the price for the eternal life they would receive.

Gerbole testified to others about his experience with God and the truth he had embraced by quoting the following Scripture: "We did not follow cleverly invented stories when we told you about the power and coming of our Lord Jesus Christ, but we were eyewitnesses of his majesty. For he received honor and glory from God the Father when the voice came to him from the Majestic Glory, saying, 'This is my Son, whom I love; with him I am well pleased.' We ourselves heard this voice that came from heaven when we were with him on the sacred mountain" (2 Peter 1:16–18).

Since Christian faith is lived out daily, Gerbole stayed there for one year, sharing with people about his walk with the Lord, praying for the sick, and making peace between persons who were in conflict, and in this way served both God and man. And the voice of God continued to encourage him, saying, "Do not be afraid. I am with you."

After living in this way in the house of Anbessa Aga for one year, Gerbole returned to his parents' home in 1975, as directed by the Lord. Since they had not expected that the weak boy who did not have shelter would live this long, they had decided to bring closure to the matter. They were in the process of preparing a memorial meal (*tezkar*), with an ox ready to be slaughtered. When he arrived unexpectedly, they were in tears and amazed as they received him. His mother and uncle, who were at the forefront of pushing the idea of bringing closure to the situation, were very happy. The meal that was being prepared was used as a welcome banquet. People feasted, rejoicing in the fact that "he who was declared dead has come back."

As days rolled by, situations went back to their original status, and the conflict between light and darkness resurfaced. The family was on edge about the boy. Some even wished that the plan for the memorial meal (*tezkar*) had succeeded and closure had been given to the fate of the boy. It became apparent that declaring the death of this boy was not an easy matter. That he was not dead was fine, they thought, but had anything changed in his life? So they asked him some questions as a test. "Has your thing left you? Where were you? What about the person who used to talk to you—did he leave you, or is he still there?"

Gerbole's response was one short answer for all the questions. "He has not left me, and I am still like before." All stared at him in bewilderment. Because their stare was intimidating, Gerbole, not knowing what to do, went to a corner and kneeled down to pray. His family, who were sitting around the fireplace, left the house, fearing that he would curse them. He continued to pray alone in the house.

At this time, as he tended to lean more and more toward prayer instead of talking, they became afraid of him. Because of that, they did whatever he asked without hesitation.

In country life, no member of the family lives without working, so Gerbole contributed by looking after the cattle and the sheep. Each Tuesday, he walked for three hours to the chapel at Mogor and participated in the overnight prayer. He spent the day, while on his job, in prayer and fasting.

Meanwhile, the struggle within the family continued to gain strength, like fire covered by a pile of ashes. Every Tuesday, when he came home with the cattle, they would add more chores on him, thinking he would be tired and discouraged and stop going to the chapel. When it got dark, it got so pitch-dark that one could not see anything ahead. In this way, they were trying to weaken him.

In fact, he had encountered problems on two evenings. One evening, after one hour of walking, the darkness became worse, and the road was muddy from a recent rain. In occasional flashes of lightning, he saw that four hungry hyenas had encircled him. He had to do something quickly. This boy had only one choice. He said, "Lord, chase these hyenas away from me."

He stood still and waited in the dark to see what would happen. He could only know the result when the next lightning flashed. And when it flashed, all the hyenas that had encircled him had disappeared, and he was able to resume his journey. At times, when he was not able to follow the narrow trail, he would stop and wait for flashes from the sky, filled with peals of thunder. Then, he would adjust his path and continue. Finally, he arrived at the life-filled chapel at Mogor.

The other difficult evening was during the dry season, when there was no rain or hyenas to deal with. His family had purposely tried to delay him until it got dark by giving him a series of assignments, some important and others not so important. Furthermore, walking in the forest doubles the darkness. Accustomed to asking help from his friend whenever he faced problems beyond his ability, he said, "Lord, you have said let there be light in the darkness. Please light the way for me." Immediately, a beautiful light—different from the sources of light he knew—descended from above. The surroundings were lit up like day, and from inside the light, a voice came: "Do not be afraid. I am with you." The light that came down was living and walking with Gerbole. As he continued his journey, he watched nocturnal wild animals running here and there, frightened by the unexpected light.

That night was the first time the glory of God came upon him and touched him. As soon as he reached the chapel, floating in joy and happiness like one would float on air, that light filled him with the Holy Spirit and left. In order that the new thing he received would not be taken away from him, he immediately went to the sheep pen and began to pray in tongues and rolled in a manner he could not control. He would stand up and jump up and down. At times, he would kneel down. He spent the night in this way, and in the morning, he went to where people were praying. Since his clothing was covered with the dung and urine of the sheep, the best option was to stay away from people and let his clothes dry in the morning sun. He spent a good part of the morning doing that. Meanwhile, at intervals, he tested if his new language and power were still there. It was not only that the glorious light had visited that night, but it had passed to all those in the chapel. As a result, many were also filled by the Holy Spirit.

"You, O Lord, keep my lamp burning; my God turns my darkness into light" (Psalm 18:28).

And then, like before, Gerbole's family and the people of the community began to hate him again. That they were on the verge of performing the funeral in his absence meant that they really didn't want him to be there. With one accord, they said to him, "You are different from us and cannot live among us. Go away." That was 1977, and a spiritual conference had been organized at Moga, about one day's journey from Ebentu, where Gerbole was living at the time. In those days, it was the practice for people to prepare their provisions and walk for two or three days to attend conferences and partake of the blessings of God. Upon the invitation of believers, Gerbole joined a group and traveled to the conference, where he stayed, sharing the food of the people who took him. But he could not find anyone who would offer him a place to live, so he had to head back to the people who hated him and who did not want anything to do with him.

When Evangelist Deresse Geleta traveled to Agamsa for ministry, he took Gerbole along and introduced him to Brother Amsalu Kefyalew, a farmer by trade and one who served the Lord as a singer. Evangelist Deresse said to him, "This boy is innocent and humble and was evicted from his home because of his belief in the Lord. In time, he will develop into an important man of God. For now, let him help out here and live in this house as your son."

After he gave this charge, Evangelist Deresse left for home. On the trip to Agamsa, Gerbole had to be carried across the Horagonka River by someone because he was not able to do it on his own. However, even though this boy needed someone's help to cross a river, he was a strong soldier of the Lord.

Singer Amsalu Kefyalew was not new to Gerbole, because he had seen him ministering at the Moga conference. In fact, he had wished that the Lord would give him an anointing like Singer Kefyalew and expressed his desire to serve the Lord in the ministry of singing, because he himself was very much blessed by this ministry. And indeed, Gerbole had served in singing during the beginning of his ministry.

Since the level of persecution was lower in Agamsa as compared to Ebentu, believers moved to Agamsa. Gerbole met Desu Sori and Tolesa Sori, who had left Ebentu and had become refugees. They lived in someone's home and worshipped the Lord in exchange for doing household and farm chores. These three cared for and comforted each other.

While Gerbole's main job in Brother Amsalu's household was tending the herd, on his way home in the evening he would gather and bring in firewood. It also was his job to wash the feet of the family every evening. But the most difficult responsibility was fetching water from the river and filling the tank for the cattle. Since the herd was large and Gerbole's muscles were weak, it took several hours to complete this tiring job. This kid was really weak—as he grew up, he barely had sufficient food to fill his belly, let alone build his muscles. He had never experienced family love, never had a full stomach, and was always on edge and always fearful. His body was emaciated as he moved from place to place as a refugee. He was just skin and bones.

People who knew him then said he was so weak that he did not even have a firm grip on his herdsman's stick. This kid was expected to spend the whole day watching the herd and performing chores after sundown—all on a meager breakfast and the little food he was served in the evening.

During his stay in Agamsa, the days were filled with loneliness and hunger. He experienced scorching heat from staying in the sun; cold during the rainy season, as he did not have adequate clothing; and feelings of being a foreigner. He felt that quitting would be abandoning the Lord, so he persisted in doing what was impossible and lived under these circumstances for three years. His compensation during the three years was limited to being able to freely worship the Lord. He went to church every Sunday. Every evening, after Gerbole washed Mr. Amsalu's feet, Mr. Amsalu would read to Gerbole from the Bible, and it pleased him very much to hear the Word of God. He usually requested that Mr. Amsalu read the Word, and because the man loved the boy, he gladly did that for him. He drew the boy close and caressed him as he read to him. Mr. Amsalu loved Gerbole more than he loved his own children. When Mr. Amsalu returned from trips, the first person he would ask about was Gerbole. The responsibilities this boy had were heavy, not because they hated him but because the nature of rural life was like that. Gerbole said that everyone ekes out an existence in this way.

"What I learned from living there is faith, persistence, and patience in times of trouble and hunger. After staying the whole day on the food I ate in the morning and feeling famished, nothing would be served to me when I got home in the evening. I would wash the feet of the family members, handle the calves and sheep, and herd them into their respective pens. Finally, I would enjoy listening to the reading of the Word of God by the elder. Then I would eat supper and go to bed. And the voice of God used to come to me always. The Lord used to comfort me by saying, 'Do not fear; all this will pass. It is to teach you and not because I forgot or abandoned you.' And I drew comfort from the Lord's words of encouragement."

Toward the end of the 1960s, a great revival started in Amuru, Kiremu, and Agamsa as a result of the movement of the Holy Spirit. Even witch doctors and sorcerers abandoned their practiced and ran toward the Lord. In every rural community and village, the saving power of Jesus Christ was manifested clearly. Those possessed by evil spirits shrieked and were delivered, even before they arrived at a conference site. One of those whose life was impacted by that heavenly visitation in 1970 was Amsalu Kefyalew, and he accepted the Lord through the ministry of Dr. Haile W. Michael, a US-based international evangelist, teacher, and leadership trainer.

As time went on Mr. Amsalu became strong in the Lord and served through singing. Mr. Amsalu remembers the condition Gerbole was in when he came to live in his house as a refugee. He relates his experience like this:

> Gerbole was at an age where he could not work and support himself. He was thin and weak, covered with scabies, and full of sores, and because his hands were shaky, he could not even hold a stick. I said to myself, if God gave him to me to serve him as a father, I will accept the responsibility and welcome him with love. And truly, I came to love him more than my own children. Every evening after washing my feet, he would ask, "Are you tired?" When I would tell him no, he would then say, "Read the Bible to me." He used to love very much hearing about the faith heroes and fathers like Abraham,

> Moses, David, Elijah, and Daniel. He was ready to serve everyone and never said no to anybody, and so people gave him the nickname "Mr. Yes." He and his friend Negera used to run barefoot in thorny bushes to exercise their faith. While Negera's feet used to be bloodied, no thorn would touch Gerbole's feet. After three years, he had to return home because the Lord told him, and we saw him off reluctantly before fully savoring our relationship with him.

Toward the middle of 1978, the voice that had directed Gerbole all along told him, "It is enough now. Leave." While the family and the community at Agamsa loved and embraced him, he decided to return to his parents at Ebentu. He joined the believers in that community. Instead of spending his days alone with the cattle, he communed with the faith community. He was free to participate in conferences and go places. He ran errands for leaders from one church to another. At a time when there were no phones in the area, Gerbole became a swift message carrier. When spiritual conferences were held, he washed the feet of participants, fetched water from the river, and helped ready food supplies and other things. In this way, he emerged on the scene and transitioned to the wider ministry that the Lord prepared for him. As God's time for ministry had arrived, his feet were ready to move in any direction.

CHAPTER 5

THE BEGINNING OF MINISTRY

The government issued a directive that no one should just sit idle; people had to work or go to school. This message filtered down to the community level and farmers' associations. As a result, Gerbole, from the Horocho community, was sent to school. The Galilee Elementary School accepted him as a second-grader, and he went to school, while living with believers. Since there was no postal or phone systems, he became the preferred person and the swiftest means to carry messages from church to church and between leaders. He enjoyed this and got excited when sent in this way. He would travel through valleys, cross mountains, and traverse thick forests and arrive at his destination swiftly. As a result of his service, church leaders and ministers came to know him better. And in the school he became a likeable student, both in the eyes of the teachers as well as students.

As a result he was elected as a leader—Gerbole Hirpa, leader of the second grade. *Pentes* (evangelicals were referred to as Pentecostals) were not liked at the time, but this second-grade leader was well liked. Just as God was with Joseph, when He helped him serve as a slave and in prison, the hearts of both the teachers and the students at Galilee Elementary School became open to this "outsider," who in turn enjoyed their favor. The lesson from this is: if only God is with you, all else will fall into place. Because God was with Gerbole, everybody, big and small, accepted him.

Because he reflected the fear of the Lord, everybody noticed this boy. His homeroom teacher, Mr. Getachew Jalo, was impressed by his character and loved him. Gerbole's spiritual life influenced his teacher to come to the Lord later in life.

During the three years he was in school (1981–83), in addition to his studies, he began to minister and gained experience. Even though he was a leader in his class and a favored student, he would take time off when ministry came his way. Sometimes he would disappear for as long as a month or two or even more before resurfacing again. Because he and his activities were well known, both students and teachers never uttered anything to him other than "welcome back." At that time, he went beyond serving his community. Traveling beyond the horizon, he crossed the Blue Nile River to minister in Gojam Province. He and a minister called Diriba Tola were sent out after they knelt down and the leaders of the church prayed for them. In those days, the leaders did not give provisions to those they sent, because it was said, "Do not carry spare clothes or a purse." They simply said, "God be with you," and sent them off. In those days, the only things supplied to those sent on mission were handkerchiefs for wiping their sweat, candy to keep their mouths refreshed, some change (about fifty cents in United States currency in the 1970s), and a flashlight with batteries. These were the only things these two were given. As Gerbole looked back to that era, he said, "What we could get from the trip never crossed our minds. In fact, ministry and benefits were never thought of as related. The main desire of our hearts and our prayers was the flowing of the Holy Spirit, the salvation of souls and the end of persecution."

They began their trip from Galilee, passed by Ende, cut across through Kelo, and reached the lowlands of the Nile valley, which is the land of the Gumuz people. They were given food and shelter by the Gumuz, and after two days' stay, they crossed the Nile River on rafts.

As soon as they crossed over to Metekel in Gojam, they made their base in the home of believers in Bulen and Dibate and preached the gospel to surrounding communities. The Shinasha believers dressed them to make them look like local people. Many people believed in the Lord Jesus Christ and were saved. Many sick people came, carried by others. The ministers did not do long and formal prayers; they said only, "Be healed in the name of the Lord," yet the sick were healed instantaneously.

Since the Lord was with these youth, many miracles and wonders happened. And they encouraged the community of believers and healed the sick. After six months, as their stay was coming to an end, a rumor reached the provincial youth league office that *Pentes* who crossed over from Wollega were spoiling students. The provincial youth league secretary, along with concerned officials, accompanied by soldiers, began to canvas the area. When they finally learned where the ministers were, they rushed directly to that village. Gerbole and Diriba had just returned from a ministry and were having a meal, believing the surrounding area was at peace. As the Scripture says, he who watches over Israel does not slumber or sleep. The voice of the Lord whispered into Gerbole's ear, "Eat quickly and get out."

"Eat quickly—the Lord has told us to leave from here," said Gerbole to his friend Diriba. They quickly said good-bye to the host family and headed to the Nile gorge at breakneck speed.

> If the Lord had not been on our side—
> let Israel say—
> If the Lord had not been on our side
> when men attacked us,
> When their anger flared against us
> they would have swallowed us alive;
> the flood would have engulfed us,
> the torrent would have swept over us,
> the raging waters
> would have swept us away.
> Praise be to the Lord,
> who has not let us to be torn by their teeth.
> We have escaped like a bird
> out of the fowler's snare;
> the snare has been broken,
> and we have escaped.
> Our help is in the name of the Lord,
> the maker of heaven and earth.
>
> —Psalms 124:1–8

Not long after that, the house where the ministers had stayed was surrounded. Because the wanted persons were nowhere to be found, the authorities rounded up and imprisoned fifteen leaders of the churches in the community.

The year-end general exams were fast approaching when Gerbole returned to his Galilee Elementary School after six months of ministry travels. He returned to his class and to his leadership role. Generally, it was his practice to delegate his leadership role to his trusted friend. His friend performed his leadership responsibilities without being challenged by anyone and handed back the delegated power to Gerbole when he returned. Gerbole was able to pass to the third grade even though he had not attended most of the classes that year.

In 1982, Gerbole and Diriba were sent again to Metekel and Dibate. They crossed the Blue Nile River by using the rafts of the Gumuz people. When they reached Dibate, they found that the leaders who were imprisoned had been released, the church had grown and expanded, and the believers had been transformed in their faith and love. Their ministry became very successful, and the distinctive thing about this ministry trip was the outpouring of the Holy Spirit and the infilling of many believers.

The rainy season started early while they were there, and the Nile River swelled so that their return was blocked. Therefore, they had to try the alternative route via Addis Ababa. And to do that, they needed to walk to Chagni, where they would be able to get public transport to Addis Ababa. The problem was not walking for more than sixty miles but the fact that the desert-like area was infested with venomous snakes, cobras, and scorpions. How could one avoid the scorpions when walking on foot? The snakes also shot in the air like lightning. But without God's will, the snakes and scorpions had no chance, and Gerbole and Diriba were able to traverse the area without incident with the help of a brother called Habte Gerbi, who knew a shortcut. They reached Chagni after two days and settled in a lowly motel in that dusty and hot town. Gerbole, the man of God, could not sleep, even though he was tired. Because the voice of the Lord had said to him, "Do not sleep. They will come and take you in three to eight hours," he waited in prayer without locking the door of his room.

"Lord, do not hand us over to evil," he pleaded. "Even if it is Your will that we should pass through a difficult situation, please increase Your grace for us." At 2:00 a.m., the motel where they were staying was surrounded by over twenty fully armed community revolutionary guards and soldiers. Because Gerbole and Diriba did not have ID cards, they were taken to the police station, escorted by armed guards and subjected to heavy military drills that lasted for many hours. Pushups, sit-ups, walking on knees, and sliding on one's chest were the nonstop instructions they had to obey until the sun came up.

When the commander came to the station mid-morning, he stared at them for some time and asked, "Why did you come?"

They responded to the commander, "Since the Nile is overflowing, we could not cross over to our area, and we came this way to go back home through Addis Ababa."

He then asked them, "What made you cross over from Wollega to Gojam in the first place?" They replied that their purpose was to preach the gospel. The commander, who could not reconcile their youthfulness and the purpose of their trip, assessed that they were not dangerous and released them. He said to them, "Now I will release you. Go back to your locality via Debre Markos and Addis Ababa, and do not come back here again." With a spirit of compassion, he told them, "Do not be afraid," and he sent them off to the bus station, accompanied by soldiers who would help them.

Gerbole and Diriba, who expected to be thrown into prison, instead headed to Addis Ababa, with their transport cost covered with the money given to them by the church in Dibate. They crossed the overflowing Nile River not by a reed raft of the Gumuz but over the bridge built by the Italians, and they reached Addis Ababa by way of Selale. They then embarked on their journey home, but the balance of their funds could only take them to Gedo,195 kilometers from Addis Ababa. Since their money was completely depleted, they left the highway to Nekemte and turned right on the footpath that led downhill from Gedo to Fincha. From Fincha, they traveled up the escarpment through Jarte Jerdega, preaching the gospel and praying for the sick. They reached Amuru after many days. From Amuru, they proceeded again downhill and, walking along the side of the escarpment, reached Kiremu. Then they passed through Kokofe to Gida and on to Ebentu, all the while visiting and encouraging believers. Thus, they reached home, completing a full circle. Although they traveled three days by car and ten days on foot from Chagni to Ebentu, their overnight layovers during the walking part of the journey were under trees, out in the open. Since their feet were extremely sore, and they could not travel far, it was with great difficulty that they were able to make it home.

After a couple of days of treating his feet with salt and water, Gerbole returned directly to Galilee Elementary School, where he was a third-grade student and the monitor. He was able to study the remaining time and pass to the fourth grade.

Toward the middle of 1982, the wife of Alemayehu Bayisa, their teacher, got seriously sick. As an educated person, the teacher could not just wait for his wife's recovery or death, as the farmers in the community would. He felt that she should be treated at the mission hospital, a day's journey away. So he arranged for a mule to take her and chose mature and responsible students to go with her. Gerbole was one of those trustworthy students. An experienced traveler, he did what he would do for any trip. He took his handmade towel and Bible and reached the school compound early in the morning. His towel was big and was especially made for him by a weaver by order of Brother Amenu Negassa, who noticed that Gerbole did not have anything to use on his ministry trips. While they were readying the mule, Gerbole noticed that the cushion on the saddle was not enough, so he covered it with his multicolored towel. Then the wife of Teacher Alemayehu was helped on to the mule, and the journey to the clinic started, with part of the group leading and others following.

When they reached Kiremu in the evening and were unloading, Gerbole's towel was nowhere to be found, as it had fallen off on the road. The group started to pray about the lost towel that same night at the location where the patient was staying. At that time, the patient shrieked and was delivered of demons and healed. The following day, she returned home instead of going to a doctor.

In those days, lost-and-found announcements were made at school flag ceremonies, and the loss of Gerbole's towel was announced, with the request that anyone who found it should contact the school. The story of what actually happened from the time the towel disappeared until it was found was known only at a later date.

A man found the towel and took it home. Each time he put it on, it felt like fire, and his body felt a burning sensation. Since the experience was strange and he could not use the towel, he sold it to another person. The purchaser, who thought he got a good towel for use both day and night, felt torturing pain, like the piercing of needles, whenever the towel touched his body. On top of that, a person appeared every night and tormented him, saying, "Return the towel of my servant."

The man said to himself, "If I cannot use it, let me at least get my investment back," and he sold it to a third person. The third person also sold it to a fourth person, and in this way, the news of the towel that disturbed the peace and health of many reached the ears of Teacher Gemechu Feyisa, who had made the lost-and-found announcement at the school. When the teacher went to the house of the man who had the towel, he found it hanging on the fence, because nobody would touch it. The last person who owned it told the teacher to take it, and he did. Gerbole was told the news, and he went to claim his property. Those who had mockingly said, "If your towel is found, you are indeed a man of God, and we will be like you," were convinced and came to know the Lord. They feared the Lord and honored His servant. His persecutors also restrained themselves.

Gemechu Feyisa, who pursued the trials of the lost towel, as well as the problems it created, broke the good news to Gerbole. He stated the following: "I came to know the Lord in 1976 when I lived in Kiremu. I announced the loss of the towel at the school flag ceremony and requested the students let me know when they hear news about it. After a lot of follow-up, the Lord let it fall into our hands."

Although there were people who liked Gerbole when he was a student at Galilee Elementary School, there also were those who hated and persecuted him. A person who served with him and shared his troubles during his years as a student had this testimony:

> Gerbole and I became acquainted around 1976. He came from a large family, who hated and persecuted him at a very young age. He grew up in the homes of believers. When the gospel came to our area, we were worshiping under trees, and our minister was called Seketa Geleta. Gerbole was just a little kid at the time and was serving us in singing. Since ministry was not considered a job and it was not possible to be unemployed, we enrolled in a school, just to have student identification cards. We used to go to school by day and minister during the night. We worshiped and read our Bibles in the woods and secluded places, and when people came by, we claimed we were studying. Our persecutors used to follow us all the way into the woods. They thought we were behaving in that way because of ignorance and used to give us lessons to enlighten us. But they were angry when their indoctrination did not make a noticeable change in us. The change they expected in us was denying the existence of God.

When we told them that we would not deny God, they started to take harsh measures, believing that if teaching did not change us, force would. We heard that a decision had been made to arrest us and throw us in jail. While the decision was to arrest us on a Wednesday, something happened on Tuesday night that reversed the decision. A severe diarrhea epidemic broke out overnight and killed three people. This changed priorities for Wednesday, as government officials and authorities of the revolution became involved in activities to contain the epidemic. This situation gave us breathing space, and we were able to go to school without fear. Since the school did not have toilets, classes were stopped, and students were ordered to dig toilet holes so that the disease could not be transmitted by flies.

As teachers could not supervise the digging, it became necessary to give the role to students who were able to discharge the responsibility. Gerbole and I were selected for this leadership job, which we started right away. We classified people by type of activity between those who would get hoes and shovels from home and those who would dig, and the toilet was readied. But since the epidemic continued to spread and became elusive, the focus shifted from us to the diarrhea epidemic, as our persecutors were pulled in various directions, following up the occurrences

> and reports of the disease. That we were assigned our job on the day when we were going to be thrown in jail reminded us that the God who reversed the decision against Shadrach, Meshach, Abednego, and Mordecai was also with us. That built up our faith.

The persecution that started in 1983 continued to strengthen in intensity and as such, it limited the ministry and operation of the church, even if temporarily. The church leaders stopped some ministries and reduced the number of evangelists and pastors. A meeting of leaders and ministers was held in Jale, and their ministry and life testimonies were evaluated, and unwanted workers were terminated. It had been confidentially decided that Gerbole would be among the first group whose ministry would be terminated.

His youth was considered a weakness, and it was thought that he would not be able to serve at this difficult time of persecution. It was therefore decided that he should go back home and grow up, so he was removed from ministry. The congregation wept when they heard the decision to stop Gerbole's ministry. They felt that he would never go back into ministry again, because his family would not allow it. This placed him between two difficult situations.

Gerbole posed a serious question: "I left home because of persecution, and my family will not accept me if I go back. If both my family and the church reject me, where then should I go?"

The church leaders' final word was, "You bear the situation that prevails within your family and live there. We do not have any position for you." It was a heartbreaking time for the boy. It meant sitting idle after passing through all that hardship to start his ministry, which included crossing the Nile.

After spending some time in prayer, sorrow, and silence, he returned to his parents' home. They welcomed him with joy, as was customary for them. They took good care of him, even if it was for a short time. They even gave him a plot from his father's land and said, "You work this land to support yourself, and if you want to get married, we will marry you off."

His answer about the proposal was, "What I have is just one Bible. There would be no woman who would marry me, because I do not have resources. Unless she is handicapped, how can a strong, healthy woman get married to me? What would attract her, and what would she eat?"

At that point, something was ignited in his heart, and he remembered the girl who had once said, "Even if this boy is poor and does not have shoes, I love him more than you folks, because the grace of God is on him." However, the girl was part of a family with whom Gerbole stayed on one of his ministry trips, and what she talked about was spiritual love, not romantic love.

"Lord, is my getting married my brother's concern or Yours?" asked Gerbole in prayer. And the Lord made it known to him that it was indeed His will, and the girl who kept coming into his thoughts without any competition was none other than that light-skinned beauty, Adanech. Derese Geleta, a minister of the gospel, said to him, "Since her family loves the Lord, they will not turn down your request. Even if you have nothing, they understand that you have the Lord, who is above everything else, and they will not use earthly possessions as a yardstick. I myself will go to the family with a few people and put the request before them on your behalf."

A few days after that, Derese Geleta organized a group of elders and went to see the family. The elders said to the family, "Gerbole, who visits your home for ministry, is requesting your daughter's hand in marriage, and we are asking that you would give your consent."

Adanech's family gave their consent without hesitation, for they had seen Jesus in Gerbole's life and not his poverty. This happened because the Lord was with him, and their marriage was planned from above, with the full knowledge that she would be the shoulder that would bear the burden and hardship of this servant of God.

In the meantime, the intensity of the persecution began to increase in 1984. Christians were rounded up and imprisoned, and Bibles were burned. At that time, worship services were held in the inner parts of homes or deep in the forest in secret, and Bibles were kept in beehives. Gerbole wrapped the Book, with which he had not parted for many years, with a plastic sheet and placed it in a beehive on a tree, with a parting word: "Oh gospel, Word of God! Good-bye until the day we meet again."

When Gerbole was with his parents, his main persecutor, who fished him out from anywhere and handed him over to the authorities, was none other than his own brother Hirpa. Hirpa had Gerbole jailed many times in Horocho district. Since this was a district where an order had been issued to shoot and kill any Christian on sight, Gerbole was imprisoned many times. Their method of tying people to trees for up to three days and nights—on the assumption that a person would deny his or her faith when he or she was subjected to extreme hunger—had not forced any Christians to abandon their faith. After spending seven days and seven nights in prayer and fasting, Gerbole was on his way to meet with believers when party members arrested him. (Incidentally, a huge church has been erected on the site of that district prison where Gerbole was incarcerated.)

At the time, anyone who hunted down Christians (or *Pentes*, short for Pentecostals) and turned them over to the government administration was promised a gun. Consequently, it did not take Hirpa much time to hand over his brother Gerbole. Hirpa returned home, rejoicing, with his gun on his shoulders.

At another time, two militiamen came to set the house on fire, because it was felt that this kid had disturbed the peace of the area, but he left the house and went his way. They warned him, "Disappear from here, and don't ever return."

"Where would I disappear? This area will be filled with the knowledge of God," he told them. The militiamen despised and insulted Gerbole, but he simply said, "May God be with you," and he left them. But those militiamen went beyond persecuting people; they challenged God, and they paid for it. One broke out with boils at seven spots on his body, while the cattle of nother one became blind. A son of one of the men died; some of the militiamen just disappeared into thin air. The chairman of the community association, along with two others, became followers of Jesus.

Of all the hardships Gerbole faced, the most serious one was being stabbed with a spear. The spear was stuck in the back of his head, and he lay on the ground, unconscious. Blood gushed from the wound and covered the area. His assailant left, thinking Gerbole was dead. As no one dared to come close to him, dogs licked his blood.

After three days, he got up and went to where believers were. The wound on his head healed slowly, but it left a hard, circular scar that is still there as a reminder of that experience.

All those who formerly persecuted Gerbole have now become followers of the Lord. A huge church for thousands of believers has been built where his blood was spilled. He was invited to attend a conference, at which his former persecutors asked for his forgiveness. Indeed, he has forgiven and blessed all those who persecuted and hated him. Some of his persecutors were struck with sickness, and their cattle were unable to reproduce, or they urinated blood, but when he forgave them, their blessings were restored. And all the people in the area who had attacked him now asked each other for notification if Gerbole came by, so they could beg his forgiveness.

His brother Hirpa, who handed him over for imprisonment in exchange for a gun, became sickly. His wealth was depleted, and his household was hit with extreme hardship. Later, with the counsel of others, Hirpa was able to say, "We could not get rid of that person through persecution. We are the ones in the wrong. How can one person survive when the entire community rises against him?"

Hirpa thus confessed and honored the God of Gerbole. He gathered old clothes and rags that Gerbole had left at home and hung them up for blessings on his kraal and farm fields. Then his health was restored, his herd was blessed more than before, and his harvest of crops multiplied many times over. When people asked

Hirpa about the difference in his life, he replied, "I had quarreled with God, but now I am reconciled."

We have to forgive those who have wronged and hurt us, because if we do not, God will not forgive them either, and they will not receive redemption. Therefore, because Gerbole forgave those who persecuted him, God also forgave them.

"Though I walk in the midst of trouble, you preserve my life" (Psalm 138:7).

Gerbole talks repeatedly of how God protected him, from childhood to adulthood, through many hardships and from death. When he was a youth and was preaching the gospel to all those he met, he continued to travel farther and farther away from his area, until he reached the hot lowlands of the Nile Valley. He found himself in the midst of people with cultures different from his own. In one culture, when a young man approached a girl for marriage, he had to demonstrate his readiness in a practical way. He had to kill four or five men from another area and take off their skin, from their foreheads to the pelvis, and line up the trophies in his compound. The girl to whom he proposed would then inspect the trophies, after which she would say, "Truly, this is a man, and I will marry him." If, however, he did not kill and hang up the required trophies, she would say to him, "You have not even tested yourself that you are a real man. How dare you ask me to marry you?"

Embarrassment like that was like a death sentence to the man, not because she did not accept his proposal but because her response affected any future proposal he might make to anyone else. People would say, "Aren't you the person who such-and-such a girl said that you are not a real man and turned you down?" Such a statement slammed the door on his future chances. Therefore, before a man began his quest for marriage, he had to do sufficient killing and display his trophies.

The gospel does not choose locations, as it is a message sent to the entire world, and it is preached in the city, country, and marketplaces. And that is exactly what Gerbole did when he reached the edges of the Nile, as he headed to a house and gave his greeting.

An old lady came out and after looking him over from top to bottom, she invited him into the house. "Come in," she said. "My son has gone out to look for trophies to show his fiancée because he wants to get married. He has not yet killed enough people, and he will kill you if he finds you. Let him kill another person and complete what is required of him, because I do not want you to die. He will definitely kill you if he comes while you are here. So go to the river, and pick cotton for me." She showed him her plantation off in the distance.

The cotton plantation was near the river. The heat of the sun was severe, and the ground was hot like a skillet. The soil was sandy, and scorpions surfaced here and there from under the sand.

There was hardly any place to set one's feet. Gerbole would feel scorpions beneath his bare feet, but they did not sting him. Wherever he stepped, it was the same. On top of that, the stalks of cotton were covered with fine prickles that stuck to his hands. The prickles were really sharp and pierced like spears.

In addition, the Nile was not a peaceful place. It had active hippos with loud noises that sliced the water like lightning, churning the river and creating wide swaths of foam. The army of hippos not far from the cotton picker shook the surroundings, including the picker. Those who watched the hippos needed to also focus on another army—an army of crocodiles. One could see crocodiles basking in the sun along the riverbanks, with their mouths open for the birds to pick their teeth. Everything that the great Nile contains is great—the hippo, the crocodile, the scorpion, and the cobra, which slices through the air like a missile. Truly, the Nile is filled with the great. With the scorching heat of the sun, death in this desert would not surprise anyone. In fact, what would be surprising would be to die slowly.

The people of the community worshipped the Nile and offered sacrifices to it in order to pacify its agents of death. And when Gerbole witnessed to an old lady about the gospel, she said, "Our god is the Nile." The Nile is worshipped all the way from Abyssinia to Egypt. The crocodile and the hippo, as well as the snake and scorpion, are worshipped along with it, as its powerful agents. Sacrifices are thrown to them too.

After Gerbole picked some cotton, the old lady showed up. "Okay, my son, what you have picked is enough. Since it is time for the young man to return, leave this area quickly, before he kills you." She sent him off after sharing some of their food. He hastened, following the path she showed him, all the while thinking about the sights and sounds of fighting animals coming from the river.

Meanwhile, it started to get dark, and when he looked around, he could not find anything. He did not trust getting close to the homes of the people, for fear of being caught in their hunting web. So he chose to spend the night in the forest, where wild animals lived. He picked a tree with a flat top spread like a bed and climbed it. As the night advanced, the night shift took over. The lion roared, the leopard rumbled, and there was movement everywhere as things became chaotic, like an open market. Gerbole did not feel sleepy, and the night passed before he could even think that there was such a thing called sleep. As it is written, "He who watches over Israel does not slumber or sleep." Gerbole returned home safely, under God's protection.

> He who dwells in the shelter of the Most High
> Will rest in the shadow of the Almighty,
> I will say of the Lord, "He is my refuge and my fortress my God in whom I trust."
> Surely he will save you from the fowler's snare and from the deadly pestilence.
> He will cover you with his feathers, and under his wings you will find refuge;
> his faithfulness will be your shield and rampart.
> You will not fear the terror of night, nor the arrow that flies by day,
> nor the pestilence that stalks in the darkness, nor the plague that destroys at midday.
>
> —Psalm 91:1-6

CHAPTER 6

Adanech

Mr. Tolera Ireso and Mrs. Bizunesh Dessalegn live in a sprawling compound in Horo Gudru subprovince, Limu district, Sipera Mitae locality, just across the Lebu River in the hilly land that faces to the east. They have established a family and live a respectable life. They have a total of ten children—three girls and seven boys. They earn their living by farming. Their major products are *teff*, corn, wheat, and barley, and on top of that, the size of their herd is not to be taken lightly.

The beehives hanging on the trees that dot the space along the river behind their backyard have helped to give their home the name "House of Honey." An added reason for naming the house "House of Honey" is the fact that no guest leaves the house without eating honey.

Adanech was the third child of ten, and there was a reason why she was given this name. When her father was a young man, some evil people fed him food that was laced with poison, causing a serious illness. He had burning of the stomach and felt terrified during the night. After living with this health challenge, his father-in-law, Mr. Dessalegn Duguma, informed him about a certain medicine. "I have heard that medicine has come down from heaven in a place called Amuru. My son, please go and try it."

Mr. Tolera did not hesitate. He prepared his provisions and headed east, accompanied by his wife, who carried with her the baby who was not even named yet. After two days of travel, they reached Amuru. Many like them also had heard the news that God had come down in Amuru, and they flocked in that direction, so they became part of the crowd. There, Haile Wolde Michael and Mekuria Mulugeta, together with other ministers, preached the gospel and prayed for the sick. The Lord did great miracles. The demon-possessed let out shrieks and were delivered, even while on the way to the location of the service. No demon dared keep still when the possessed got near the service.

Without anyone testifying that Jesus Christ saves, people communicated among themselves, saying, "God has come down in Amuru," and they continued to flock there. Witch doctors and fortune tellers abandoned their trade, releasing their control from the shoulders of those they had enslaved for a long time. Breaking and burning their paraphernalia, they ran to the bosom of the Lord. They then accepted the Lord as their personal Savior, were filled by the Holy Spirit, and returned from where they'd come to tell those who had not heard.

This family reached this place of active spiritual blessings, and Brother Mekuria Mulugeta laid hands on Mr. Tolera and prayed for him. And the Lord healed him. Mrs. Debele, Adanech's aunt, who traveled along with the father and mother, also received the Lord, left her sickness in Amuru, and returned home. From then on, the child's name became Adanech (meaning "she saved" or "she healed"), because her father was healed at that time. He had to return home and destroy and remove the many idols he had amassed during the years of his sickness. After he did this, the house became a Christian home and a church plant for the surrounding area. As with a fire that is poked and continues to burn, the surrounding people began to accept the gospel. Tolera ministered to those saved, and the believers multiplied.

Adanech remembers what transpired when she was just a little girl:

> When I was a little child, people came to our house with their sick. Our father used to pray for them. They would be healed and go back to their homes. Many times, the demon would let out a shriek and leave the person, even before he entered the house. Any time we saw a demon-possessed person shrieking, we used to be scared. Since we were children, we would go into the house, climb into our beds, and cover ourselves. At that time it was not the ministers who shouted in prayer and rebuked the demons. It was the demon himself who would shriek and shout, saying, "They are coming at me! I am burning!" A person possessed by an evil spirit was not able to stand in the presence of the ministers. The evil spirit used to say, "There is fire," wherever they stepped, walked or rested. Let alone this, the evil spirit used to shriek and leave, when the demon-possessed were told that they would be taken to the place of prayer. As

> the people entered the house to worship, their sickness would be left outside.

At that time of innocence, when there was love and oneness of heart, a time when believers lived for heavenly benefits, the Lord's hand moved openly with power, and many who had been bedridden for many years were healed. A stubborn cow that refused to be milked would give milk; a kraal infested with sickness was sanitized; and an untamed ox was broken in easily. All this did not happen because formal prayers were said; it was enough to just touch the person or animal who had a problem with a Bible. Incidentally, since many could not read, they said, "This is the Word of God" and used the Bible to invoke the power of God to remedy anything that was not normal.

At that time, God did not move because of the surroundings or who the preacher was but because fire had come down on that land. Demons shrieked even in villages, where believers passed through carrying Bibles. The Word of God was used to shake the powers of darkness from a distance, even before it was read or preached. Today as well, the Word of God is powerful, and if it appears powerless and does not seem to be effective, the problem is with us.

"The word of God is alive and active. Sharper than any double-edged sword, it penetrates even to dividing soul and spirit, joints and marrow; it judges the thoughts and attitudes of the heart. Nothing in all creation is hidden from God's sight. Everything is uncovered and laid bare before the eyes of him to whom we must give account" (Hebrews 4:12–13).

Adanech continues to describe those early days after her parents believed:

> Aside from delivering people from the bondage of evil spirits, our father used to be called to homes where women were in labor for two or three days. Those women used to deliver just as he entered the house. There was no haggling in those days, as the Lord used to do wonders just with one word or mere presence. I remember my father used to kneel and pray three times a day while doing his farm work. At that time, believers earnestly sought and loved each other. Our house was a place of healing for the sick and a place of rest for guests. Worship services for the community were also held there. Hence, we were expected to host those who visited the area for ministry. And not only that, ministers used to come just to take a break. The young boy Gerbole was among those who came to minister in 1980, and after that he used to stop by, even when he was just passing through on a ministry trip. He looked pathetic. My parents, who knew he was under persecution, used to have compassion and love for him. In fact, he had gone beyond being like a household member to being considered their child.
>
> One day, three brothers came to our house. They had consultations with my father and

> mother, and then they left. As I got bits and pieces of what transpired, I understood that the matter concerned me. After many days, when I was just fourteen, I was summoned to the main house where many people had gathered. At the time, I was baking *injera.* My brother Gemechu came to where I was and said, "Come!"
>
> I replied, "I am baking injera. Why should I come?"
>
> "Leave everything and come. We are going to sell you," he said.
>
> He hurried me, even before I had time to clean up. My father signed on a document and others followed suit. Gerbole also signed. Then they showed me the spot on the document where I should sign, and I signed. No one was talking, and I did not understand why we had to sign in complete silence. So I returned to my work, restarted the fire, and when the skillet become hot again, I resumed baking. The matter troubled me and threw me in such deep thought that I made the *injera* much thicker than it needed to be.

Gerbole, the would-be groom, thought about how he would make the money needed for clothing and other preparations for the wedding. "How do you make money?" he asked one of his brothers. The brother replied, "Gerbole, tomorrow's groom, if you go into the trading business, you will make money within a short time."

"What kind of business, and where would the capital come from?" Gerbole asked.

His brother gave him some starting capital and told him, "If you buy donkeys from Amuru and sell them here, you will make money."

It took three days to reach the donkey market in Amuru on foot and three days to return, which meant a total of six days for the round trip. When his mother heard about this business plan, she said to him, "My son, please abandon this idea. What knowledge do you have to engage in the trading business? I will buy for you the clothing and shoes for the wedding."

But he said, "No, Mother, let me do business instead of sitting idle." Because he was determined to go ahead, his mother prepared provisions for him, and off he went and speedily reached Amuru. He bought a young male donkey for twenty birr (ten dollars U.S.) and returned with it in tow after a week. He then took the donkey to the market in Berrisa and put it up for sale. There was commotion everywhere as the market heated up and buying and selling accelerated, but nobody offered to buy his donkey. Slowly, the market began to wind down as people left until finally, only Gerbole and an elderly man were left at the corner where donkeys are sold.

"Why weren't people interested in my donkey?" Gerbole asked the man. "From morning until now, nobody asked me about it. What problem could they have detected in it?"

"Was your donkey for sale?" the elderly man asked. "If it was really for sale, you should have tied a sign around its neck. You see, the difference between a donkey that is here for hauling stuff and one that is for sale is by this mark around the neck of the donkey."

Then Gerbole walked away to look for some kind of twig to tie around the neck of his donkey. When he returned, the donkey was lying down. Even if he put a sign on it now, nothing would happen, because the market had closed. He had to head back home with his donkey, but it got dark on the way, and he had to beg for a shelter for the night. And as often was the case when he traveled with donkeys, he had to spend the night outside to protect them from being attacked by hyenas.

The following day, he headed home and as he approached his home, the donkey fell down. No matter what he tried, it would not get up. Apparently, it had just dropped dead. He immediately called his brother who had loaned him the money. When the brother saw it, he said, "Okay, I have canceled your debt." But Gerbole was sad when he considered all the ups and downs he had to go through and the fruitless trips he had made with the donkey. "Lord, why didn't you tell me this business would not work?" Gerbole asked. The Lord answered, "When did you ask me?"

Adanech recalls that time of hasty preparations:

> After that, my mother made me weave various types of baskets fast. And when I asked her what the reason was, she simply said that we would take the products and sell them in the market. I knew only later that the money was to establish my new home.
>
> In 1984, a conference was held at Jebika, and my father took me along. The elders, who were responsible for matters related to our marriage, as well as Gerbole himself, were there. At the end

> of the conference they huddled with my father at a corner away from the crowd and decided that the date of the wedding would be in two weeks. My family then bought new clothes for me, although I was not told the reason. But my peers in the neighborhood told me, "You are getting married."
>
> I then asked my parents, crying, "Why do you marry me off? Is it because you hate me?"
>
> They replied, "Our daughter, we do not hate you. You are getting married because it is the rule." So I was given away in marriage.
>
> Because the groom's house was six hours away on foot, the bridal party was escorted by riders on thirty-nine mules. In our area, there had never been an entourage of such size at anybody's wedding. In fact, my uncle was so concerned about the number of guests that he thought maybe the group was made up of two bridal parties. When he asked my father whether the food and drink would be enough for everybody, my father simply said, "Invite them in. The Lord will bless what we have." Just as he said, nothing ran out, and everything was in excess of what was needed.

After the hectic activities of the wedding were over, the newlyweds, Gerbole and Adanech, began their married life on their own. He worked the land that his brothers had given him with hoes and borrowed oxen, as available. Because there was a stream on his land, he used it year-round to grow corn. But when his brothers saw that he was successful, they took away that land from him and gave him another piece that he could use only during the rainy season. Gerbole and Adanech stood on their new farm and called the name of God, saying, "When Lot took the green areas, the God who met Abraham in the arid area and blessed him is also with us." And God heard, and a stream sprung, and their land became green and suitable for irrigation.

After harvesting three or four crops from their new farm but before they had time to gather the harvest of the current season, Gerbole and his family were forced to leave the area as a result of increasing persecution by the people in the community and pressure from his own brothers. It was at 3:00 a.m. one day in 1987 that they slipped out of the community in secret, carrying their first daughter, Kenna. After staying with Adanech's parents for some time, they proceeded to Degem. The director of the Degem Elementary School knew Gerbole, and he hired him as a guard. As there was a house built for the guard, Gerbole moved in with Adanech and Kenna.

Gerbole, who was told to go to his family "and grow up," who was sent out by the fellowship of believers with lots of tears and financial gifts, had by this time completely stopped his ministry. He had traveled down to the areas lying around the Blue Nile River in the guise of a cotton-and-gourd merchant and preached the gospel to individuals he met along the way. During those years, he even preached to the trees in the forest when people refused to hear the Word of God. He would preach the Word of God that was brimming in his heart, saying, "You trees, you rocks—you will be witnesses. Tomorrow, you will be translated into a conference of people."

After he came to Degem, he started again to minister in the homes of believers during the night. And as his ministry expanded, he used the weekend, from Friday night to Sunday, for ministry and then returned to his guard duty on Monday morning. Meanwhile, Adanech substituted for him as a guard.

The school gave them a plot of land, and Gerbole planted corn. He left the job of weeding and looking after it to Adanech. It was not uncommon for Gerbole to give away his meager salary to poor people and come home empty-handed. On her part, Adanech strived to support her family by making baskets during the night under the dim light of a small kerosene lamp. Their children Adise and Yonatan were born in this compound at Degem Elementary School. Those who watched them live under these difficult circumstances used to say to Adanech, "Instead of nursing a baby on an empty stomach, why don't you return to your father's house where people are fed butter and honey."

Her answer to them was, "The Word of God does not say return to your parents when your husband becomes poor. Since our covenant is until death, I will not break it for the sake of my stomach."

Adanech did not forget what her father advised her at the time he made the decision to allow Gerbole marry his daughter. He said to her, "My daughter, what this person has is only heavenly treasure. He does not own earthly wealth. I had asked the Lord to give you someone who lives according to His Word, and he is that gift. My daughter, whatever I have is yours—be strong."

Adanech lived many years between the challenge of raising children within the environment of hunger and the pressure of those who were advising her to return home to her parents. In this, she was truly the second Gerbole. Her usual response was, "Since God knows that our house is empty, I will wait for Him."

Meanwhile, her parents would send provisions and always encouraged her by saying, "Do not be afraid and lose heart. Your husband is destitute for the sake of Christ. Do not leave him and come back."

But those who gave her evil counsel—relatives and close friends—were relentless. Worse yet, they said to her, "In the name of ministry, he travels to Addis Ababa, because he has married a city woman, but you eke out an existence in this empty house." Her direct and strong reply to them was, "If he wants, let him marry not just one but five women, and I will continue as the sixth."

In those days, salt was a very expensive commodity. The only source was the community shop, and there, salt was rationed by quota. One day when Adanech was baking bread and Gerbole was around the house, she asked him to go get their quota of salt. He waited in line for his turn and bought his quota, but as he was leaving, he saw weak and elderly people waiting in line. His heart was touched, and he shared his salt with these people. When it finally ran out, he went home empty-handed and silently sat in a corner.

"Did you get the salt?" Adanech asked. But Gerbole just sat there, his head drooping. Again, she asked, "Gerbole, did they give you the salt?" But he gave no answer. After that, Adanech, who always avoided pressuring him, stopped asking and just continued her work, as it was difficult for her to go beyond that point. In the evening, as the community shop worker was passing by their house, he asked Adanech why they had not come to the shop that day. Without even waiting for her answer, he gave her some salt for free and went on his way, forgetting completely that Gerbole had already bought their quota from him.

During their stay in Degem, the Lord sent Gerbole to Genji to visit and minister to the believers, of whom there were only seven—Arandufa, his mother, sister, and neighbors—and the journey took five hours on foot. Since the purpose of his trip was to minister to this small group of people as well as to give them prophetic words about the future, he prayed over the land and declared, "At this spot, a church will be planted," and he placed a foundation stone. He then instructed them to receive those who would come to them in the coming days. He also appointed an elder, a treasurer, and a choir from among the seven and prayed for them before he left.

Today, there is a big church at that place. As was said, the people flocked in, seeking the Lord, without even being invited, and the land became free of the darkness that covered it. Thus, the prophesy that "the people walking in darkness have seen a great light" was fulfilled (Isaiah 9:2a).

As Gerbole was returning from this ministry, he felt tired and hungry. But all he had was just one birr, and that could not buy him more than a piece of sugarcane (*tinkish*) to chew on. When the feeling of tiredness became so bad that he could no longer walk, he sat by the roadside, leaning against a tree, and took a deep breath. He then drifted into deep sleep. In a vision, a person approached him and said, "Get up, get up, and continue your journey." For the Lord had prepared in advance a place for him to stay overnight.

When he jumped up from his sleep, he saw an old lady standing close by. "Mother, what are you doing?" he asked.

"I am standing here to beg for help," she answered.

"Like you, I am hungry and thirsty also, only I am not begging like you. Otherwise, I am just as needy as you are. It is better for you to beg from the traders who are coming this way," he replied and started to leave.

Again, the old lady insisted, "I will not beg from the merchants. It is you I asked for help, and you are the one who will give to me."

"Really, I do not have anything," he said in a compassionate tone.

"Not even one birr?" she asked.

He thought, *If she can clearly see what is in my pocket, this thing must be from the Lord.* Amazed by that old lady, he took out the money, gave it to her, and continued his trip.

As he traveled, he kept thinking about the one birr. "Lord, why didn't you give her something? What do I have, that you sent her to me?" he asked.

"Through whom shall I give to her? It is only through you that I can give to her," the Spirit of the Lord replied.

"Aha! So that is why," he said to himself and continued his walk. He reached Galilee after dark. Because he'd traveled in the rain, he was soaked. and the road was muddy. He tried to identify the neighborhood he was passing through as well as the road in the glow of the frequent lightning. At 8:30 p.m., he approached a home that was closed but with flickers of light coming through holes in the wall.

He begged, "I am a traveler. Please let me in for the night."

Apparently his words reached the ears of the owners, for they replied, "We ourselves have a problem and cannot let you stay here overnight. We have a sick person in the house and are suffering day and night. You go look for a home of people who sleep in peace and spend the night there."

Gerbole tried to think. *Where did the men go? Or maybe there is no male in the house. Perhaps they are scared of me. Or is the sick person the man of the house?*

For the second time, he said to them, "Please let me in to spend the night here. I have medicine for a sick person."

Without missing a beat, they opened the door and invited him to come in. The fire was burning brightly, and he saw the owner of the house lying on a mat by the fireside. The man was not uttering a word because he was seriously sick. Gerbole, the traveler who was soaked from top to bottom, like someone who had come out of the sea, turned to the members of the family and said, "Step aside and prepare food for him."

They were not sure whether he was a witch doctor or someone else—they were confused. They could not reconcile his destitute appearance with his claim to be a medicine man. All the same, they cleared the space. Rejoicing inside that he was now closer to the fire, Gerbole approached the patient. Slowly leaning over, he spoke into the patient's ear, saying, "The Lord Jesus will save you, and your sickness will be taken away from you. Believe that he will heal you and stand up."

The person stood up as someone who just had awakened from deep sleep unexpectedly. He said, "Someone removed shackles from my ankles, and I am healed." And he began to rejoice.

The family marveled at what just happened, for the head of the house, whom they had expected to die any moment, declared, "I am healed. I am healed." Checking all the parts of his body, they embraced him with joy and began to cry.

Gerbole the "medicine man" intervened and said, "Please do not cry. Instead, bring him food." To the man, he said, "You sit down."

They all complied and brought Gerbole a blanket (*gabi*) to make him comfortable and warm water for his muddy feet. Food and coffee was served and the atmosphere in the house changed. A sleeping place was properly readied for him, and he slept. He did not stir until the owner of the house woke him up for breakfast at eight the next morning. After a hearty breakfast and coffee, they gave him twelve birr for provisions along the way and sent him off on his journey to Degem and his guard duty at the school.

One other time when Gerbole was returning home from ministry, an evil man waited for him and said, "You cadre of Pentes, you have recruited almost everybody, and there seems to be nobody to stop you. You will see; I will stop you. I will kill you."

Gerbole pleaded with him, "My brother, please leave me alone. I do not recruit people for evil but for good, so that people will turn away from their evil ways."

But the threatening man answered, "You will not live in this area while you continue to do this. I will kill you." His blood was boiling more than before as he stared at Gerbole.

While the two were still facing off, Gerbole realized that the man would not allow him to pass. So he changed his tone from begging to challenging him as an equal and said, "Please do not touch me. You will regret it."

"If I see you pass this way another time, your blood will be like that of a dog, and no one will accuse me," the man threatened.

The house of the evil man was located near this road. Since the road was the only one, Gerbole had no detours or trails to circumvent the house. It became a test for Gerbole as to whether or not he should pass on that road. If he was to minister, his only exit and entry route to and from the neighborhood was that road. Hence, if he chose to minister, he would have to take that road; if he chose his life, he would stay home. The question was, therefore, how could the servant of God, who passed through many hurdles and traps, fearfully abandon his calling for which he had committed his life? He presented the matter to the Lord: "Oh, Lord! Which way shall I pass? Please make him blind so that he cannot see me."

The threatening man became blind and entered a life of darkness. He could not know who was coming or going. Gerbole used the road again after he verified the news. It would have been good if the evil man had repented and contacted Gerbole after he was struck with blindness. But he did not do that, and he died a month later.

When Gerbole lived at Degem, he served two kingdoms. For the earthly one, he was a security guard; for the heavenly one, a minister of the gospel. In the evening after the students went home and in the morning before classes started, he would lay hands on the desks and pray. "Oh, Lord! Bless the children who sit at these desks. May the fear of You control them. May they know You and place themselves under Your control. May You make them honorable and useful to their nation."

In this way, he would commend to God those children of poor farmers. He also did the same thing for the teachers and other workers. He commended them to God and prayed that they would rid themselves of the heretical thinking of the time, be people who knew and controlled themselves, become models for the next generation, and be ones who submitted to the Lord.

Because God honors requests like this, many among those students have gone on to pursue higher education and have reached high levels in society. Many have built homes for their parents in Addis Ababa, and some have even taken their families overseas. And among the teachers, including the director of the school, many are alive and well in the Lord.

The director gave orders to the guard on duty to punish and counsel late-coming students. As counsel precedes punishment, Gerbole would say to the late students, "Receive the Lord if you love Him. He loves you and will make you a good and great people." He would then say that they had received the necessary counsel, and he would send them to their classes. There were those who deliberately came late to school, just to hear his counsel daily.

Although his title was security guard, his three-year stay in Degem was a time when he returned to ministry. During the night he made his ministry rounds in the area, and on weekends, he traveled farther afield to serve. He would preach in empty classrooms as if they were filled with people. Furthermore, he prayed for sick students, their parents, and other people in the community. Some distressed people would carry their sick to where Gerbole was, and the Lord healed them.

CHAPTER 7

Another Big Job

One night toward the second half of 1989, Gerbole and Adanech had an identical dream. In the dream, three men dressed in white came to their house and said, "Your time here has ended, and it is enough. There is another big job prepared for you, and you will go there."

While the husband and wife were wondering about their dream, Gemechu Tolera, Adanech's brother, arrived, bearing a message from the Nekemte Full Gospel Church. The leaders of the Nekemte Church, like Pastor Tesfaye, had apparently been looking for a minister with a vision and a call from the Lord. And then they heard about this person called by God but hated by people, who earned his living as a security guard at a school. It was at that point that the messenger was sent to call Gerbole to the Nekemte Full Gospel Church. The transport money for Gerbole was donated by Pastor Tesfaye from his own pocket. Gemechu Tolera, who had employment, covered his own expenses. Together, they traveled to Gida.

Since this was the confirmed will of God, it did not take Gerbole long to move from Degem to Bekaqechu. Qechu was a village established during the villagization program of the *Derg* (socialist) government, but since the farmers slowly slipped out of the village and moved back to their former homesteads at Koye and Qosi, there were many empty huts. Gerbole and his family moved into one thatched-roof house. He left his family in this condition and headed to the church in Nekemte that had invited him to come. There, they welcomed him with love, prayed for him as a minister, and gave him whatever support they could afford, and then he went back to Qechu.

Life in this village was a challenging one for Adanech:

> I gave birth to my fourth child, Martha, here at this village, where there was not even a bed. On top of that, the house leaked because it was built hastily by government order, and those who built it just did the basic work to save themselves from the abuse of the political cadres. As a result, there were times when we used to pile all the clothing on the children to keep them warm, and Gerbole and I covered ourselves with curtains. When it was time for me to have the baby, Gerbole had to minister at the conference in Shambu. Even if he had decided to stay home, I would not have allowed him to do so. Therefore, the only option left was for him to pray that I would not have the baby before his return. He left and came back after a month. I was in my tenth month, with the baby still in my womb.

> Gerbole arrived on a Thursday and on Friday, I washed his clothes. He was tired and had to rest. On Saturday, after we had coffee, Martha was born at 9:00 a.m. There was no food or clothing. I spent the day and night without food and ate only on Sunday, when my mother brought me some porridge. Even under those difficult circumstances, my face looked like I had enough food and was comfortable, and the children appeared like they were well taken care of, even when they went to bed without food. I have never had a sick child or been in distress. My entire family was healthy and at peace. The only one with me when I had each baby was Gerbole. He would stand on his feet and pray, and I would go into labor and give birth. My labor was usually for just a moment, and then I would deliver and have the baby in my arms.

Gerbole, who came to be widely known as a result of his ministry, said to himself, "It is not necessary to stay in a village that people left because they hated it." He therefore found a house on the edge of Gida town for a monthly rent of twenty-five birr and moved his family into it. They also rented a bed for four birr per month. But soon after that, Gerbole had to go on a ministry trip, leaving Adanech with her four children in the new house. Her younger brother Getahun, who did not feel comfortable about her staying alone with the children, came to stay with them. The landlord kept asking her to pay the rent. But she kept telling him to wait until the return of her husband, which extended to four months. He firmly replied, "Will I lose my money if your husband does not show up? Pay or leave the house, but if you don't, I will move in my things."

His threat was not only verbal, for he soon came into the house to prepare a drink and roast grain for the moving party. The fire he built burned Adanech's all-purpose apron, which doubled as a nightgown. When she realized that she could no longer stay there, she rented another house and moved with her children.

Gerbole, who had left in March, returned after six months through Addis Ababa. He went directly to the house where he had left them. When he found out that the owners were living in it, he said, "I left my family here. Where did they go?"

They ridiculed him. "It is your business to know where your family is, and you turn around and ask us!"

Hearing this, Gerbole started searching for his family and finally found them after checking around. Adanech felt emotional and embraced him with tears—they cried together. The crying had a language of its own, as hardships and difficulties weighed heavily on them. Her children often went to bed hungry. One time, she did not have any food to give them for two days. On the third day, she could bear it no more. "Lord, will these children have to bear this a third day? Please pass by my house," she prayed.

While she was pacing back and forth, not knowing what to do, a man called from outside. He was passing by with a loaded donkey when the overfilled sack on the donkey's back began to spill the grain. He said to her, "Please give me a container to reduce the load, because it is spilling and giving me a problem."

He then reduced the load by about ten kilograms and said, "Toast this for your children." He thanked her and left.

And she thanked the Lord, who is always close, and took the grain inside. That corn served as their provision and miraculously lasted until Gerbole returned.

It is likely that Gerbole also worried about his family wherever he was. Once when he was in Addis Ababa and had attended services at the main Full Gospel Church, he thought of his family more than at any other time. He became emotional and headed to the men's room, though he had no need to go to the toilet. He needed to grieve before the Lord. "Oh Lord, here, they have a place like this just to relieve themselves, while my family has no decent dwelling. Please give me a house."

The following day, a certain man of God called and gave him 1,500 birr. And with this big money in his pocket, an amount he had never handled before, he was reunited with his family. Since this money was a direct result of his prayer for a house, his heart was not open to sharing with the poor, as he had done. He had received it for a specific purpose. When he heard that the house Adanech rented was up for sale, he asked the price. They told him it was 1,500 birr. So the price of the house was set in Addis Ababa, and the decree was issued when he groaned in the toilet. He bought the house for the exact amount he was given—not less, not more. For the very first time, they became home owners.

This house was on the road that led to the central market. As a result, those going to and from the market passed by their house. It was soon evident that some services were expected by the culture. Those who were late in starting their journey would ask for shelter for the night; thirsty folks would ask for a drink;

the sick would appeal for a place to rest. Some would even tether unsold animals to the fence, requesting that Gerbole keep them until the next market day.

If anybody who was running late in the evening stopped by at any home in the neighborhood, they would be directed to Gerbole's home. People in the area would say, "They love guests." Therefore, any person unable to continue his journey because of darkness would stand at the entrance and say, "For the sake of God, please allow me to spend the night at your house." Sometimes other guests were already in the house, and the big problem was space and food. For sitting, they used the stump of a big tree, which was kept outside at night. As for food, if they had nothing to offer, they would just pray and give the guests water to drink. They would simply say, "Our food is this water. Please drink." There were those who drank that water and were met by the Lord in their dreams; they went home as believers after hearing the message of the gospel. If we see the continuous flow of guests from this perspective, we can conclude that this happened so that people would know the way of salvation.

Once, within the first few years after they moved to Gida, Gerbole felt hungry while returning from a ministry trip to Chelia. A lady called Kemila was selling tea and bread under a shade tree on the side of the road. He decided to take a rest. Taking him for a customer, she immediately served him tea and bread. Since he had no money, he said to her, "I am a traveler and do not have money. Would you give it to me for free?"

"Are you a beggar?" she asked.

He answered, "I am not."

"Declare you are a beggar, and you will eat," she insisted.

At that point, he remembered how food offered at a time of hunger degraded Esau:

"Once when Jacob was cooking some stew, Esau came in from the open country, famished. He said to Jacob, "Quick, let me have some of that red stew! I'm famished!" Jacob replied, "First sell me your birthright." "Look I am about to die," Esau said. "What good is the birthright to me?" But Jacob said, "Swear to me first." So he swore an oath to him, selling his birthright to Jacob" (Gen. 25:29–33).

Therefore, instead of saying, "I am a beggar," Gerbole chose the reply Jesus gave when He was hungry—"Man does not live on bread alone."

So that it would be a lesson to all those who would be tested to change their identity for bread, he stuck to who he was—an evangelist, not a beggar—and continued his journey with his dignity intact.

As Gerbole had to pass through a mountainous area, he said to the Lord, "Since I have refused to be called a beggar and missed the opportunity to get food, please give me something to eat." He met a group of people chewing on sugarcane (*tinikish*), and one of them gave him a piece of his cane and said, "You traveler, you look hungry. Here, take this. Wet your mouth with it."

Gerbole continued his journey chewing on it.

People who go to the market do get thirsty, so anybody requesting a drink of water at the Gerbole home drank water fetched from the river by Adanech herself. The women in the neighborhood all drew water from the well in their compound. But Adanech somehow could not master the art of drawing water from the well. And so she would pick up her huge earthen vessel and go down to the river. But the most difficult situation for them was their hungry children, who eyed the loads of bananas carried by people heading to the market. They would stop and have a drink, but they rarely offered bananas or sugarcane to the children, whose hungry eyes followed them.

As a result, Adanech and Gerbole did not like the house at all. With a united voice, they prayed, "Lord, this house is next to the road, and we are tired of hosting so many guests. Now we have reached a point where some have to sleep outside. Please give us a larger house."

During the night, they heard a noise as the rain was coming down. Something happened that shook the house. "Could it be thunder?" Gerbole whispered to Adanech in the dark. Whatever the case, he picked up his flashlight to go outside, but he could not locate the door. The layout of the house was not like before; it had changed. He found a hole to slip through toward the back. As he inspected the outside of the house using his flashlight, he discovered that a tall eucalyptus tree had fallen on their house. The trunk, branches, and leaves had completely demolished the house and flattened the roof to the ground. The part of the house still standing was the corner where the family was sleeping. The house they bought with prayer was, overnight, demolished by prayer. Even though the owner of the fallen tree offered to pay them for the damage, they refused to take the offer.

"The previous owners of the house were interested in buying back the property for the same price they sold it to us—1,500 birr. We took the money and left," Gerbole has said.

They agreed that the new house they would build should have three rooms to accommodate the many guests who streamed by.

They presented their prayer of faith in this way. They put one birr's worth of nails, three wooden poles, and three birr on the ground and prayed. "Let the nails search for the corrugated iron sheets and all iron-related materials, the poles look for wood, and the money search for more money. In this way, let them all come together and be a house." In less than a year, all the materials came together to be a three-room house.

In 1991 many people were flocking to the Lord as a result of the visitation of the Holy Spirit, but at the same time, the Enemy was trying with all his might to smother the heavenly fire that could not be stopped. Wise ministers, who understood that God was leading them, organized a huge conference at Beka. The conference was planned under the cover of Evangelist Gemechu Tolera's wedding. Although he had been married already, it was simply used as a dramatic act to be a cover for the conference at a time when such meetings were outlawed. Many traveled for two to three days with their provisions to participate in the conference at Beka. Since that was during the final days of the *Derg* regime and mass movements of people with their provisions were suspect, many were detained and released on the way to the conference. For instance, a pastor called Iyassu was detained, investigated, and flogged twice during his two-day journey from Bello to Beka.

Other participants from all directions had to pass through various hurdles to get to Beka, where the glory of the Lord was manifested. A choir had come from Nekemte, the capital of the region. The preachers were evangelists Argaw Nida, Taddese

Aweke, and Getachew Haile. When the provisions the participants brought ran out, the organizer slaughtered three oxen to feed the people. It was a time of huge revival, one that did not stop, even after the conference was over. That revival gave birth to a brand-new church—Goshen Full Gospel Church.

CHAPTER 8

The Works of Faith

> For this is what the Lord says: You will see neither wind nor rain, yet this valley will be filled with water.
>
> —2 Kings 3:17

This man of God, Gerbole, started his trip on foot from Gida through Nekemte and stopped for breakfast at the Ephrem Hotel, located in the thick forest of mango trees within the Didesa Valley. He then continued his journey slowly to Ghimbi on a bus that struggled to climb the Abasenan escarpment. Beginning from Ghimbi, he ministered anywhere and everywhere the Lord led him, both in churches and to individuals along the route. He skirted Dembi Dolo to the left and followed the road to the right. When he reached Mekenejo, he followed the road to Nejo and Mendi. He then crossed the Dabus River, the wide tributary of the Blue Nile, on a temporary metal bridge, and reached Bambasi in the Benishangul and Gumuz region. After ministering to the saints in Bambasi, the Lord led him to Begi.

The distance from Bambasi to Begi is just sixty kilometers. The road was built during the Italian occupation (1936–41) and has been in use without any maintenance, in spite of its being rough, rocky, and muddy.

Once in a while, one finds Russian-made public transport vehicles with high clearance running on that road, but the fare they charge is unheard of anywhere. I remember traveling on this difficult road on a truck that was loaded with freight that I was able to find through a middleman. The price was exorbitant, and the experience very difficult. Even though we paid the hefty price, we passengers spent the day pushing that heavy Italian truck out of the mud until we reached Begi.

Unlike now, when many roads have been built, travel in that part of the country then was very difficult. Today, it is easy to travel from Bambasi to Tongo, as well as from Bambasi to Begi, and on to Chanka via Gidami, Jimma and Horo. Previously, there was a time when we had to pay five hundred birr to travel from Begi to Gidame, a distance of fifty-six kilometers. And that was not even a regular public transport vehicle but one that belonged to a mineral exploration project of the Ministry of Mines. The driver did that on the side to help people who desperately needed transportation.

At another time, I remember traveling by air from Addis to Begi by a light airplane and from Begi to Gidami by a mule that was sent by the church. The mule became weak and quit on me, and I had to find a place to stay overnight at a believer's home, with the help of the deacon who had brought the mule. We reached Gidami mid-morning the following day. Such a journey, which was very difficult for me, was one that Gerbole traveled on foot.

On average, the average person can walk seven kilometers per hour, and based on this, the trip from Bambasi to Begi took Gerbole one day and a half. The believers in Bambasi escorted him to the edge of the town and then returned home. He passed through the flatland, with corn and sorghum fields to the left and right, and reached the dense bamboo forest of the warmer climate. But he could not withstand the hot sun of Qeshmando. It was so hot that he could no longer wear his shoes. He took them off and as he was trudging along through what was called "Monday Market," the Lord spoke to him. He told Gerbole to give the suit he was carrying in his bag (to wear during times of ministry) to the two ministers who would meet him in Begi—the jacket to the one who would meet him first, and the pants to the one who would wash his feet in the evening.

It was difficult for someone who was just arriving from a very difficult trip, with bruised feet and extreme hunger and thirst, to give his clothing to others. But to this servant, who obeyed God and who God himself trained, obedience was a joy. He handed over the jacket and the pants to the persons, as he was instructed. At the time of this writing, the person who received the jacket was serving as a singer, while the foot washer who received the pants was ministering in Addis Ababa.

When Gerbole started thinking about the return trip after ministering for two weeks in Qelem and Begi, he could not imagine going back the same way he'd come. He thought instead of flying from Begi to Addis and went to the airline office.

It was unthinkable to expect a direct service from the small airline office in Begi. It was a must for coffee merchants, who shipped their coffee by truck to Addis Ababa, to reach there before the arrival of the shipment. So they needed to visit the airline office, as would those who had to travel for medical reasons. To these were added other travelers, and the number of potential passengers exceeded the seventeen seats of the small aircraft that served the route. Now, in a situation where there was no road and the chance to fly was limited, it is possible to guess how the airline representative would choose his passengers, given the way things are done in Ethiopia. Whether it is the person who has shipped a truckload of coffee or the patient who is desperate to save his life and is looking for a physician, both are ready to pay what it takes, legal or illegal, to get seats on the flight.

Gerbole's plan was to fly to Addis and then travel by bus to Nekemte to reach home with fewer difficulties. At the airline office, he said to the agent, "I would like to travel to Addis Ababa. Please give me a ticket."

"It has been many days since the last flight, and there is no flight today," responded the proud and sole employee in the office.

Like Gerbole, others had come to inquire about flights but continued to hang around, in spite of the fact that they had been told there would be no flight that day. Gerbole thought for a moment and then took out two ballpoint pens, rubbed one against the other, and talked as if the pens were a mobile phone. "Hello, Addis Ababa. Hello, Jimma. Can you hear me? Hello, Addis Ababa. Isn't this the airline office? Please send an aircraft urgently. We are many in a difficult situation and are waiting for you." Then he said to the passengers, "Wait here. The airplane will come today."

The airline agent tried the radio communication equipment to check whether or not the flight was coming, but it was not working. Nobody believed what Gerbole said.

For the second time, he repeated, "The airplane is coming today. Let's go to the airport."

One of the passengers sneered at him. "Do you know more than the employee of the airline?"

However, those who were ready to believe anything because of the intensity of their problem begged the airline agent to keep trying the radio communication. After lots of attempts, a voice was heard from Addis Ababa, confirming that there was a flight to Begi that day. Gerbole got a ride to the airport in a car that was dropping off another passenger, and he flew to Addis Ababa.

CHAPTER 9

The Ministry of Foreknowledge

> Though the doors were locked, Jesus came and stood among them.
>
> —John 20:26b

In Nejo town, where Chombe lives, the people turned against him. He earned his living by running a hotel. But people from every walk of life declared that no one should enter the doors of a hotel run by a "Pente."

Chombe had word that the prophet would be passing through his town. So when Gerbole arrived, Chombe told him that the community had rallied against him to the point where his hotel had to be closed. He requested that Gerbole pray that God would intervene on his behalf.

Gerbole said, "I have nothing to say to you now, but the Lord will give me a word when I return."

On his way back, although his bus ticket was for his entire trip home, as he neared Chombe's town, Gerbole asked the Lord, "Shall I continue my journey, or shall I get off?"

The Lord's response was, "Get off and give him a solution." Getting off the bus, he asked a shoeshine boy (who usually knows such things), "Where is Chombe's hotel?"

It did not take the boy long to give him an answer. "Oh, it was closed a long time ago."

"Why was it closed? Did he become bankrupt?" Gerbole inquired.

The shoeshine boy explained the details. "Since he is a Pente, anybody who entered his hotel was condemned, and as a result, people stopped going there. Because of that, his business died, and he had to close it down."

"Can you show it to me now?" Gerbole requested, and as an encouragement, he gave the boy more money than his shoeshine charge. The boy took a shortcut to get him to Chombe's hotel. Sure enough, when he got there, he found it was closed, just as he was told.

Chombe and his wife were in their bedroom, crying before the Lord. Gerbole explained why he'd come—"It is the Lord who sent me." He then uttered what the Spirit of God gave him. "May the Lord enter this closed house. Let any curse that is inside come out. Let there be peace in your house and in your life and business." He stayed overnight in that closed hotel, comforting and talking to them. In the morning, he said to them, "Now the Lord has come to your closed house, and you must clean up, put things in order, and restart your work."

According to Gerbole's instructions, they reopened the hotel for business. Now all the people, who were told by the Devil not to go, started to flow in, because Jesus told them to do so. Their work became more successful than before.

Currently, the hotel is prominent in that town, and the volume of business is more than could be handled.

"The words of him … who holds the key of David. What he opens no one can shut; and what he shuts, no one can open" (Rev. 3:7).

At another time, Gerbole traveled from his home in Gida to Nekemte on his way for ministry. As usual, he made arrangements for a hotel room for the night to enable him catch the early morning bus. Then, he stopped at his barber for a haircut. Right in the middle of the haircut, a message came to him from the Lord. He had to go to someone known to him in a hurry. Since he did not know the address of the house, the barber agreed to take him there. When he got there, the house was closed. He went close to the door and sat there, leaning against the wall.

"Get up, and let us go. There is nobody here," said the barber.

"Since the Lord who led me here knew the house would be closed, I will stay here, but you go," Gerbole replied.

The barber then left for his shop.

Dr. Makonnen, the owner of the house, soon returned with his family. He later explained:

> The people in the community do not like us because we worship the Lord. As a result, people who were looking after our son when we were at work laced the drink in his bottle with poison in a manner we least suspected. After that, he could not hold down his food and in fact, I am surprised that he did not die. But he could not get well. We were in great difficulty, as we could

> not say whether he was alive or dead. It was in the midst of this that Prophet Gerbole searched for our house and came at God's instruction.

They opened the closed house and carried the unresponsive child inside. While the members of the family were crying, the servant of God took the child in his arms and paced around, praying in tongues. The soul of the child came back into him, and he began to stir. He was healed. He opened his eyes and began to play.

"The spirit of death has left your home. Praise the Lord," Gerbole instructed.

He bid them good night and gave the child over to the parents. He did not accept their invitation to stay overnight and have a meal. He said, "I came just for this—I was not instructed to eat, drink, or stay overnight."

At this writing, that boy is a fifth-grade student.

Teacher Negese Oliqa and his wife, Bachu Akuma, who live in Asosa, had been married for over five years, with no children, even though the cultural expectation for a married couple is to bear children. Slowly, their love began to grow cold, and clashes would occur from time to time. As if that were not enough, the wife fell seriously ill one night. She bled continuously until the bed and clothing were soaked in blood. The husband tried to do whatever he could all night to help her. Sometime toward dawn, they heard a knock on the door. (Actually, in their difficulty, they should have knocked on someone else's door. Instead, they bore this extreme difficulty alone through the night.)

It was the Lord Himself who knocked through the servant he sent. "Please open the door for me. It is Gerbole. I came sent by the Lord," he told the man. When the teacher opened the door, Pastor Kelifa Elias and Gerbole were standing there. As soon as they entered, they moved directly to the bed. But the teacher tried to invite them to sit down so that they would not see the blood-soaked bed.

However, Gerbole approached Bachu and said, "I came because God sent me. Do you believe that the Lord Jesus can heal? Please get me some oil."

When they gave him the oil, he anointed her and prayed. "After this, you will see no bleeding. Next year at this time, you will have a baby," he said, and they left.

The bleeding stopped as soon as the ministers left the house. Exactly a year later, Betselot Negese was born, just as Gerbole had said. As of 2011, Betselot is a young girl in the ninth grade and a member of the church choir.

When Gerbole traveled to Asosa in the Benishangul Gumuz region in 2007, he said to Pastor Yohannes, "Please call in all those believers who desire to have children but are barren, because the Lord wants to visit them."

The pastor contacted by phone or sent messengers to all those who had problems having children and invited them to his house, where the minister was staying. Gerbole prayed for them. Among those who got children were Asfaw Mamo and Rahma Temam. They named their child *Bereket* (blessing).

It would not be proper to transition from the stories of Asosa without recording the testimony of Pastor Makonnen. Even though Prophet Gerbole and I have ministered together since

1991, it is not possible to relate everything in detail. But I will mention a few of those who stand out for the glory of the Lord and as testaments to the fact that the minister is a true servant of God.

One day, a lady came to the home where we were staying and said, "My husband is not a believer but worships the Devil. He forces me to prepare sacrifices that he offers to evil spirits and as a result, my soul is troubled. Please pray so that my husband will believe."

Gerbole said to the deacon who was with us, "Bring some firewood," and when he did, Gerbole placed it on the table. He asked the woman the name of her husband. When she told him, he said, "Believe that this firewood represents your husband, who is not here."

"Okay, I do believe," she said.

Then he turned toward me and the deacon and asked, "And you two—do you believe?"

Looking at the firewood, the deacon laughed, belittling the idea. The prophet said, "Just as the Lord Jesus kicked out all those who laughed when he was raising the dead girl, you also get out, because you laughed out of lack of faith."

The prophet, the lady, and I laid hands on the firewood on the table and then put it in a corner. After two days, the unbelieving husband came to the house where we were staying. We told him the story of the gospel and discussed with him areas where he had questions. After he understood the truth, he agreed to accept the Lord. We had not understood who he was until that moment. But when the owners of the house said, "This person is the one in whose name you laid firewood, and you prayed for him," we praised the Lord in amazement. The lady also came the following day and told us that her husband got up at 3:00 a.m. and said, "Let us pray and sing a song for me."

That story helped many to grow in their faith and convinced unbelievers to be saved.

There was a season when I was under the attack of the Enemy, and things were in chaos. One time, when the prophet Gerbole visited Asosa for ministry, he came to my house and said, "The Lord has sent me to pray for you." After he prayed for me and my wife, he declared that God had broken the work of the Enemy. He said, "Let us go out of the house so you will get a sign and believe. You will see a snake and kill it."

The three of us, including my wife, went out of the house. Gerbole said, "Here comes the snake. Kill it." We crushed and killed it.

Beginning from that time many complicated schemes of the Enemy unraveled, and things began to improve and become normal, just as the man of God had said.

One time during the reign of the *Derg* (the Communist government), we were invited to pray for a baby girl who was sick. The mother had been a believer before but had backslid and married an official of the government. Because the child could not be healed through medical treatment, the mother wanted to try the Lord she had known. Her husband, who was a member of the Communist Party, gave her permission.

Gerbole started by sharing the Word, but he stopped in the middle and said to the husband, "God is saying the child will not die, but you will die within a few days unless you give yourself to the Lord right now." When the man heard this, he was gripped with fear. "Now, if I pray for you, and you repent, the child will be healed and death, which is standing outside your door, will go away, embarrassed and empty-handed," added Gerbole. Right away, the husband repented in tears. The child was also healed, and the mother returned to the fold.

There was a time when we were in Dembi Dolo for ministry and a phone call came from Gedo around 10:00 p.m. There was a police officer who had been a believer but had later grown weak and abandoned his faith. He was seriously sick and had been admitted to the police hospital. The doctors had advised his relatives to take him home alive, rather than carrying his corpse, and that was what they had done. At that point, they telephoned the prophet Gerbole for prayer support. After Gerbole prayed for some time, he said to the relatives, "Please give the phone to the patient."

One relative said, "He is not able to move. He is at the final stages, and it has been twelve days since he's had any food. He was on glucose, and he is now off that and cannot talk."

The prophet said, "Hold the phone close to his ear." He told the man important messages, including that he had run away from the house of the Lord. After that, the patient, who appeared to be unresponsive, started to cry out loud. And then Gerbole commanded him, "In the name of the Lord Jesus, get up and walk." Surely, just as he was told, he got up and started to move about in the midst of those who were attending to him.

The relatives of the sick person and others from near and far who had come to visit him were utterly amazed at what happened in front of their eyes. Those who were believers praised the Lord and jumped for joy. The rest, in deep amazement, shifted their eyes between the bed where the patient had lain and the healed man who was walking among them. The man was still holding the phone to his ear.

Gerbole said to him, "Now you go eat some food and drink some soda, and call me after thirty minutes."

The man, who had been close to the brink of death and for whom the undertaker had been ready, called after half an hour and said to the prophet, "I just returned after seeing off my relatives and neighbors."

When the prophet and I heard this report on the phone together, we glorified God.

My wife had a tumor in her uterus and suffered for fourteen years. Finally, we learned from the doctor that it had become cancerous. As a result, we had to travel from Asosa to the Black Lion Hospital in Addis Ababa many times. We used to do two or three trips a year. Since traveling by road was difficult and not comfortable for a sick person, we had to travel by air. And then, after all that, to learn that it had developed into cancer made us feel hopeless.

Finally, the doctor told her that they would operate on her after five days. Since the situation weighed very heavy on me, I called the prophet and told him the difficult situation. Gerbole called two days before the scheduled date of the surgery and said, "God says no knife will touch her. The sickness is no more there. It has gone away. Go to the hospital tomorrow and confirm this. I will come to see you tomorrow, and we will praise the Lord together."

As instructed, we went to the Black Lion Hospital on the day of the appointment. The doctor did all the final checks that needed to be done prior to surgery. As he reviewed the results, he talked to himself in a confused way. He looked at my wife and then went through her thick medical file several times, comparing the files with the clean results of the tests.

"It is amazing," the doctor told her. "The final result does not show any type of cancer in the uterus. Since you are completely healthy, you do not need the surgery. Go home in peace."

"How is this possible, Doctor? Weren't you the one who told me that it had become cancerous?" my wife asked.

"Yes, I did say that to you," the doctor said, "but now it is not there. Just as you believed you had sickness for fourteen years, today convince yourself that you are healthy and go home."

And truly, after that my wife was completely healthy.

One time when I stayed at Prophet Gerbole's home, he ministered to various people continuously for many hours. His wife, Adanech, and I noted this and turned off the phone so he could get some rest. But around 10:00 p.m., he begged us to let the phone stay open. We did as he requested, because we felt maybe God had spoken to him. Sure enough, the phone rang right away, and when he picked it up, the call was from a family in great difficulty. Although it is not appropriate to reveal the secret of that family, we know that God spared them from destruction.

CHAPTER 10

When Obedience Bears Fruit

From the beginning, what God wanted from Gerbole was obedience, submission to His will, and a willingness to be molded. As this continued to happen, the clouds of difficulties began to slowly roll away. He started to live better in terms of food and clothing. He had two complete suits and wanted to add one more.

"Lord, give me one special suit," he asked.

The answer was not long in coming: "You will give even the ones you have to Arega and Haile."

Right away, Evangelist Arega and Evangelist Haile entered the house, making their greetings heard as if they had been waiting outside.

They said to Gerbole, "We are on our way for ministry, but we need suits to appear before the people. Please pray so that God will provide for us."

But Gerbole said to them, "I will not pray, because God has already prepared the suits you want. Why pray for something that is already done?" He then took out his suits and gave them one each. He also had one hundred birr in his pocket for his own trip to Nekemte, but the voice came again: "Give them fifty birr each." He did all he was commanded and proceeded to the bus station to travel to Addis Ababa empty-handed.

In his pocket he had just one birr. Gerbole said, "Even if there is no money in my pocket, God is on His throne."

He boarded the bus headed to Nekemte and sat in seat number one. As the bus started to roll, he surveyed the back seats to see if there was anybody he knew, but there was no one. Deep in thought, he leaned against the window, as he felt sleepy. The bus conductor started to collect the fares and would have begun with seat number one, but he moved to seat number two, planning to later collect the fare of the sleeping passenger. He collected the fares all the way to the last seat. On the second round, he gave back the change he owed to passengers, canceling the figures he had noted on the back of their receipts. He also had to handle the embarking and disembarking passengers, and that increased his load. When they reached Gutin, the passengers had to get off for breakfast. Then Gerbole thought of something. He said to himself, "Before the conductor embarrasses me further down the road, let me try to find believers I know and pay him."

He went to the assistant, who was guarding the door of the bus until the passengers returned, and said to him, "I have not paid the fare."

The assistant quickly responded with good news. "Someone paid for you and got off at Andode."

"What kind of a person was he?" asked Gerbole.

The assistant simply said, "Why should I care about the looks of the person? I do not remember his face."

Gerbole wondered, "How could a person pay when he was not on the bus from the beginning? Was he just a human being or an angel?"

He took out the one birr he had in his pocket and changed it into coins. He then put fifty cents in one pocket and the remaining fifty in another pocket, declaring, "Let these one hundred cents be one hundred birr." He bided his time, pacing back and forth on the road until what he declared came to pass. While he was doing that, a couple traveling from Dade to Addis Ababa but staying overnight in Nekemte saw him on their way to their hotel. They took the initiative to call out his name, and they exchanged greetings.

"Please, let us have lunch together," they offered.

Gerbole thanked them but politely declined the invitation. "No, I am waiting for someone. Please go ahead and eat, and may the Lord bless you," he said and stepped away.

The husband and wife consulted each other, gave Gerbole one hundred birr, and left. Now that the one hundred cents had fulfilled their work, he gave them to beggars and replaced them with fifty birr notes.

The following day he traveled to Addis Ababa, arriving toward evening. Since he got word that Evangelist Gebru Woldu was looking for him, he got in touch by phone, and finally they met. Gebru said to Gerbole, "Brother I was looking for you urgently, and now I have found you. When I was in Germany recently, people asked me whether I knew a servant of God who needed help. When I told them I knew of an evangelist called Gerbole, they asked me to carry this to you." He handed Gerbole the gifts. Evangelist Gebru said that in addition to the gifts, the donors had pledged to send Gerbole 100 euros by way of monthly support, which was an encouragement to Gerbole. That support continued for some time.

The servant of God, who gave away his suit in Gida and carried his spare shirt and socks in a plastic bag, headed home from the bus station with his gift from overseas. After he and Adi (short for Adanech), his wife, thanked the Lord for what had happened, they opened their gift and found several suits, shirts, and ties for Gerbole and a sweater and jacket for Adi.

Incidentally, it was not without generously giving of herself that Adi received these gifts. When Gerbole told her that he had given his suits to people, she told him, "There is no problem if God commanded you to do that."

Following that, a lady who was Adi's supplier of firewood said to her, "Please loan me your dress, as I do not have any to wear when I go to the market." Adanech had therefore given out her best dress and had nothing left in her wardrobe, just like Gerbole.

A true believer obeys God. And an obedient believer can command God. God also obeys the believer. God will fulfill the requests of a person who believes and obeys, because his requests are on matters related to the glory of God. This has nothing to do with those shallow people who rush to make themselves rich by saying, "God has said, 'Command Me, and we will command Him,'" before they submit their spiritual lives to the kingdom of God. But the heroes of faith have "through faith conquered kingdoms, administered justice, and gained what was promised; who shut the mouths of lions, quenched the fury of the flames, and escaped the edge of the sword; whose weakness was turned to strength; and who became powerful in battle and routed foreign armies" (Heb. 11:33–34).

Concerned by his mother's advanced age and her persistence of unbelief, Gerbole prayed, "Lord, the years are increasing, and my mother is not saved yet. How long can she stay without coming to faith? We could separate suddenly. Please do something while we still have this opportunity in our hands."

The Spirit of the Lord said to him, "Use your authority."

Then Gerbole thought, *If I am allowed to use my authority, miracles will happen in whatever I say, and that means she will believe miraculously.*

His mother was very scared of snakes. Gerbole said to Adanech, "Today, a snake will come to my mother's house."

"I am concerned it might bite her," she said.

"I said it would come but not that it would bite. It is not allowed to do anything beyond scaring her."

Adanech begged him, "Please don't shock her."

Since they lived next door at that time, and Gerbole knew that a snake would come, he was hanging around in the neighborhood when his mother let out a shriek. Adanech ran into the mother's house and he followed.

"What happened?" he asked his mother.

"A worm entered my house," she said. She had the habit of referring to a snake as a worm because of her fear of it.

To give weight to the situation, Gerbole said, "Don't say worm; say snake."

His mother begged him, saying, "Don't call its name; it will bite me."

He replied, "Believe in the Lord Jesus Christ so that it will not bite you. I told you many times, but you refused. Now, if you do not believe as a result of this one snake, there are many on the way from the river."

She said, "First, take out this one, and I will believe."

He said, "No problem, but you kneel down here and Adanech will watch so that it will not bite you." The snake had stuck its head in a hole as soon as it came in.

They agreed to use the snake as a weapon to chase the forces of unbelief, so his mother knelt down, Adanech became a guard, and Gerbole used his authority to lead her to repentance. The process of crossing over from death to life was completed. The sins of Mrs. Terefech Begna were washed away by the blood of Jesus, and her name was written in the Book of Life. There was joy both in heaven and in Gerbole's hut.

When his mother stood up from where she was kneeling, she pointed to the snake and said, "Now take it out for me."

Even though they tried with a rag to pull out the snake, the head snapped off and remained stuck. Since nothing could be done to take it out, they poured kerosene into the hole and set it on fire and left it. In spite of the fact that it was set on fire, the elderly lady created a problem by saying, "I will not spend the night in this house unless the remaining part of the snake is taken out."

Gerbole then said, "Mom, that is okay. What you are afraid of is not the part that is remaining in the hole of your house. That piece has no life in it. Since you have done what we said, we will also do what you are saying. Even if it is just for you to see, it will come out. Just wait a little." She was given a seat outside until she was able to see the dead piece revived.

Despite the fact that kerosene was poured into the hole where the part of the snake was stuck and then set on fire and the hole closed, the mother pressured them, saying, "Unless it is taken out, it will bite me." Because of this, Gerbole and his wife decided to do whatever the mother said so that she would take responsibility for her own soul.

"Please, Lord, let this piece of the snake come together if it is broken into pieces and be revived if it is dead. Let it somehow come out here from where it is so that she can have rest," Gerbole prayed. After a while, the part of the snake dragged itself at the pace of a worm and was seen in the compound. They handled it with a stick, but it did not defend itself or run away. Apparently, it just came to be seen. In fact, it died right there. So they threw it away with a stick, and the old lady became free and entered the house.

Another time Gerbole took a rock and threw it on another rock and said, "So-and-so's heart is broken," mentioning the name of the person he wanted to accept the Lord. After some time, that person was passing by Gerbole's home. They greeted each other, and he was invited to come into the house. Because Gerbole had said to the chair, "Do not release him to go until his heart is broken," that person sat there for a long time, listening to what Gerbole was telling him.

"I cannot go. My heart is broken," the man said.

"If your heart is broken, get up and go," Gerbole told him, and holding his hand, he raised him to his feet. That person, an official of the government at the time, came to faith that day.

Sometimes Gerbole traveled back-to-back to minister in many churches. Once he started at Ghimbi and went on to Nejo, Buke, Mendi, Asosa, and Begi, and as he was returning, the Lord commanded him to minister to the people at Qiltu Kara, a little off the main road. Word got out that the man of God had come, so the people pitched a tent in the compound of the chairman of the church leaders, where he ministered to them. The following day, he was waiting for transportation when the Lord revealed to him two needy persons, and he heard a command: "Give them half of the three thousand birr given to you by the churches you ministered to."

He went to the homes of the two persons, gave them the money, and boarded a bus headed to Ghimbi. There, the Lord showed him a family that needed prayer and commanded him to visit them. He left his bag in a brother's store and went to the house. The Lord said to him, "Take out what is left in your pocket, and give it to them."

It was two months since he had left home. The needs of his home, his children's requests, his travel requirements to get home—all these required money; yet he gave to them, in total obedience, as always, to the voice he heard. He took his bag from the store and stood by the roadside. "Lord, give me a car to take me, or give me money for transportation," Gerbole prayed. Just then, a Toyota Land Cruiser stopped right in front of him. He knew the people in Gida. They exchanged greetings, and they invited him to get into the car if he was headed to Nekemte.

They traveled to Nekemte together. There, one said to him, "You are returning from a trip," and invited him to dinner and paid for his hotel room as well. After spending the night in the same hotel, they asked him whether or not he was proceeding to Gida.

"Yes, I am," he said, and they gladly took him home.

After Gerbole greeted his family, who were longing to see him, Adanech said, "Since the neighbors will definitely come when they hear about your return, give me money to buy coffee, if you have some."

Gerbole was perturbed. He could not find anything when he checked in all his four pockets except two birr, that had been overlooked, stuck in one of the pockets.

"Here, use this for the time being, and later more will come," Gerbole said.

Due to the intensity of the pressure on him, he looked for a secluded place to pray and went into the bedroom. At that time, a person looking for Gerbole's home arrived in front of the house. The man entered the house and said, "A person in my dream told me you needed money and instructed me to come and give you this."

The money he handed to Adanech was double the amount Gerbole gave out to the two families needing help. After giving the money, the person said, "Tell Gerbole to come to my house when he is done with his prayer time."

When Gerbole came out, relaxed, from his bedroom, where he had been hiding from the problem rather than praying, Adanech told him what had happened. He immediately went to see the new bank manager who had come to see them. Since the house of the manager was right in the compound of the bank, Gerbole located it easily.

"You, man of God, the Lord has told me that you labor for Him, and you do not have anything," the manager said. He handed Gerbole money that he had set aside for him for transport and clothing.

As he was coming out of the compound of the bank, two persons in an Isuzu truck called to him. "Please, if you know this area, would you know a man of God called Gerbole?"

He said to them, "Yes, I do know him."

"Please, can you show us his house?" they asked.

He said yes and hopped into the truck. When they got to the gate, he said, "Let me check if he is there," and he went into the house. He quickly came out and said, "He is in. Come in."

The men came into the house and sat down. Then they asked Adanech and Gerbole, who were sitting right in front of them, "This is the house of the man of God, but where is he?"

Gerbole said to Adanech, "Tell them."

She pointed to Gerbole and said, "He is the one."

They were surprised. One said, "We became like the people on the Emaus Road." They unloaded what they had brought for them by the instruction of the Lord, took it into the house, gave them some money, and went on their way. Obedience bore fruit—much fruit.

Another time, Adanech whispered to Gerbole with fear and hesitancy, sharing the pressure she was feeling. "Gerby, we actually do not have any food in the house."

She never desired to share with him about needs and shortages, because she wanted him to minister with freedom. But that day, she dared to tell him how empty the house was, how the flour container, the dough pan, and the bread basket were all bare.

He had only ten birr in his pocket. "All will come," he said, and went to the market, as if he were going to shop for supplies. It was a Saturday. It was not *teff* that he bought with the ten birr but five empty burlap bags. He prophesied over the five bags, saying that the Lord who filled the stone jars with wine at Cana of Galilee would fill these. In the evening, five donkeys loaded with five bags of *teff* were driven to the doorstep of the house. The men who brought them were ordinary farmers who knew Gerbole. One said, "We thought this would be for the children." They unloaded the bags, put them in the house, said good-bye, and left.

Generally, a person longs for food when it is not available. When it is available, questions arise related to its quality and type. At one point, the family was longing for meat. Kenna, the first child, said she was hungry for meat. The thing that triggered her hunger was hearing her father speak about God's being able to prepare a sheep for the sacrifice.

She said to her father, "If God is able to prepare a sheep, He will prepare one for me too, because I am hungry for meat."

"Yes, he will prepare one," her father responded. Now, once it is said that He will prepare, what should one wait for? They got up early the next morning, shared the various responsibilities, cleaned the house, and put everything in order.

By faith, the house began to have the aroma of meat. They bought lots of red onions. Gerbole was told not to go anywhere, and he sat on the seat provided for him. He was stressed to the point of feeling detained. He tried to pray. "Lord, what shall I do?

Do not embarrass me." He waited for a long time, staring toward the gate. "Spare me from a terrible embarrassment," he prayed.

At four o'clock, his brother, Hirpa, who had traveled nine hours, driving a huge fattened sheep, arrived. Not a believer in the Lord, Hirpa drank and smoked. At one time, when those who handed over *Pentes* to the government were rewarded with guns, Hirpa handed over his brother Gerbole to the police in return for a gun.

Hirpa said to Gerbole and his family, "I believe it was your kind of a person, fair and handsome, who in my dream during the night said to me, 'If you do not take this sheep and give it to them, your cattle will be decimated.' I was afraid, and so I came."

The long-awaited sheep was slaughtered right away, and since preparations had been done earlier, the cooking part was done within a short time. The home that by faith had the aroma of various flavors of meat during the day, began to fill up with real smells of meat. Hirpa accepted the Lord and left his cigarettes and sin in Gida.

Gerbole said, "You cannot go home in your old clothes after accepting the Lord," and he gave Hirpa his own. Hence, the brother returned home wearing new clothes. On the way there, he had come with a sheep he'd raised, but on the way back, he returned with the Lamb of God—a huge profit. The Word that was given to him as he returned home was: "It is for freedom that Christ has set us free. Stand firm, then, and do not let yourselves be burdened again by a yoke of slavery" (Galatians 5:1).

Hirpa continued his way home, repeating, "I will not return to the yoke of slavery. I will not return to the yoke of slavery."

CHAPTER 11

Enemies of Righteousness

> Now Joseph was well-built and handsome, and after a while his master's wife took notice of Joseph and said, "Come to bed with me!" But he refused.
>
> —Genesis 39:6–8

Gerbole was returning home to Gida after ministering in a town called Ande and as always, his journey was on foot. Not only he but other ministers, like Deresse Geleta, Duressa Dinsa, and Dr. Haile Wolde Michael, all covered the entire region on foot. But on this day, since there were traders traveling with mules, he begged some female traders, saying, "Please put my bag on one of your mules." They were onion traders on their way home in Gida with loads of onions on two mules.

The women looked at the young man in a flirtatious way and whispered to each other. "We will load it for you if you pay one hundred birr," they said, supposedly revealing the result of their secret.

He presented his request the second time, saying, "What I have is twenty birr. Let me give you that."

While they were hesitating, he took out the twenty birr he had and gave it to them. They put his bag on the load of onions and tied it down with a strap. When they reached the middle of the forest, after they checked forward and backward, one said, "What you have to pay is fifty birr."

He told them, "I do not have fifty birr. I have given you what I have."

"You have to pay," one of the women insisted, blocking his way.

He said to them, "If you do not want to carry it, return my money and bag."

"If you do not have money, we will give you another choice." They stopped driving the mules and came close to him. One asked, "Who is more beautiful between the two of us?"

He gave them a biblical answer: "Both of you are beautiful, because God created you fearfully and wonderfully."

One said, "If both of us are beautiful, you will choose the one you like and have sex with her in the forest."

They came much closer and cornered him in the middle. He responded by saying, "I am a married man and not a person who does such things wherever he gets the opportunity."

"You will either pay fifty birr or sleep with one of us. Choose between your options." They cornered him.

He replied, "I do not have fifty birr. I gave you what I have."

"If you do not have the money, you will sleep with one of us by force," one said in a strong tone.

He skipped to the side and said, "I will not sleep with you. Put my twenty birr on the ground and leave."

They made fun of him and in a seductive manner, one said, "Your twenty birr is now in our hands, and you will not get it. Don't try to be smart with us."

From where he stood, Gerbole said, "Let me tell you something. There was a person called Elisha, whom you do not know. Just like me, when he was traveling from place to place for a similar kind of work, children insulted him because he had no hair. 'You bald man, get out of this town,' they said. Since they verbally attacked a person who was walking peacefully, he cursed them, and two bears came out of the forest and crushed some of the children. If you do not return my money, unload my bag, give it back to me, and leave in peace, I am going to call bees to attack you."

They laughed out loud at him until their bellies hurt, and in fact, they sat down, saying, "We will see what you will do."

Gerbole backtracked a little and climbed a small tree and said, "Oh Lord, You are the God of righteousness and purity. Send me bees and save me from these ladies who are agents of the Devil and enemies of righteousness."

Three bees began to circle him just as he finished his prayer. He appointed and gave orders to the three bees. "You add a thousand more and go and sting those ladies."

How many divisions of bees they mobilized is not known, but the three bees received the orders and left. Immediately, the women rolled on the ground and shrieked with very loud voices, shouting, "Help! Help!" But no help came. The bees assigned to sting the mules did their mission so well that they dropped their load all over the place and jumped in the river and drowned. Gerbole climbed down from the tree, picked up his bag from where it was dropped by the fleeing mules, and got back on the road. A road construction crew stopped for him and gave him a ride all the way to Gida. The ladies had become unconscious, and passers-by took them to people's homes for help. After three days, they were taken home, swollen all over. After that, there was also some kind of attempt to find the person who had caused them this harm.

Two conferences were held that year at the location where the women were stung by bees. The reason that spot was chosen was because of a huge pine tree (*zigba*) that served as shade and made it convenient to sit on rocks and attend the conference. There were bees living there, but whether it was the same colony that attacked the women was not proven. The bees did not affect the believers during the conferences. We did not understand if the bees were the type that hated sin but loved songs. The conference that started under that tree at that time has become the foundation for the establishment of the Ende Full Gospel Church.

Although there were many challenges in Prophet Gerbole's comings and goings and in his ministry, his protector God was always with him, guarding him and his ministry. Evangelist Urga told us the challenge they faced when they were ministering in Amuru. Here is how he described it:

> When we went to Amuru for a conference and got to the venue, we noticed two women wearing long dresses with faces covered, along with two men similarly dressed with turbans on

> their heads, canvassing the area from a distance. We understood that this was strong opposition from the Enemy. As the prophet understood in the Spirit, these were people sent to put the assembly under bondage. He therefore raised his hands and, in brief, said, "The God of Elijah, where are you?" Suddenly, a naked, crazy man appeared from nowhere and hit the two ladies and one of the men hard and bloodied them. He then left. This happened because they were sent by the Devil and kicked against the pricks. Many people were saved and freed from demon possession, and the sick were healed. Those who were brought on stretchers walked back to their homes.

It was not only those who would pronounce curses that the Enemy and evil people prepared. They even placed people who would attack the minister with a knife in the assembly. The person prepared to stab with a knife was hired from very far and could not do anything but sit for long hours, watching what was happening. As he was closing in prayer, the prophet said, "There is a person sitting here with a knife. Pray with eyes open." He then gave an invitation to the person, saying, "You come to the office with your escorts and see me. You could not attack according to your plan and have decided to simply return home."

When we entered the office at the end of the service, the person came with his two escorts, confessed, and handed over the knife. He went home, soaked by the blood of Christ and not Gerbole's blood.

There is also Merga Jerbo's testimony that reminds us of Gerbole's ministry in Amuru:

> The community around Amuru Werebera is an area where there is a lot of witchcraft. A python is fed and worshipped, and there is lots of evil worship. I told Gerbole about this when we were traveling together. He said, "We will pray now, and you will see what will happen." We then prayed. The following day when I escorted him up to Amuru, he said, as we parted ways, "Be strong and pray. There is some big thing that will happen here."
>
> The sacrifice for the python is put under a tree called Homi. There, a lot of animals are killed, and butter, honey, milk, and any produce from the land is presented as sacrifice. If the sacrifice is not presented at the appropriate time, the python climbs a tree and makes loud whistling noises, disturbing the community. The sound is so loud that the earth shakes. It does not seem it is coming from just one python. Even the wild animals scatter when they hear that sound. A disturbing spirit comes into the hearts of people along with the loud noise.
>
> When the people of the area, led by the elders and witch doctors who know the ceremony of the sacrifice, plead, "Have mercy on us. Forgive us. We will double the sacrifice," the python calms

> down. Lots of sacrifices are presented, and the python comes down from the tree and eats from the sacrifices.
>
> Prophet Gerbole, who saw how openly Satan was ruling the land, had prayed about the situation when he spent one night at my uncle's and his wife's home—the only believers at the time, even if they were weak. He was zealous for the Lord and prayed, "May the fire of God eat this tree and these people be freed from evil, and may the church of Christ be planted in this place."
>
> This was his prayer for them as they parted. The huge, live tree dried up within that week. The witch doctor submitted to the Lord and began to preach the gospel to those he had previously misled. Through his preaching, the whole community was changed and taken over by the Lord, and a church was planted at that same place.

If we raise the issue of ministry and challenges, there is something we cannot avoid. A conference had been organized at Gori below Dembi Dolo by way of Ashi. The speaker was Prophet Gerbole. Apparently, the conference was planned without supporting it by prayer. Everything was dry and devoid of a spiritual touch.

Before his turn to preach came up, the prophet understood that the Enemy was strong and that he was going to face combat with the Enemy. He went outside the shed and was walking back and forth when he noticed a young girl at one corner, praying, falling on the ground. Since he understood that a prayer team had not been designated for the conference, he asked the leaders, "Are you not prepared with prayer for this service? And what is this girl doing alone? Is this thing only her burden?"

One replied, "We did not assign her to pray. It is about half an hour since she started, and we were afraid to tell her to stop."

"Leave her alone. Why would you make her stop?" he asked, and he went back into the shed.

When it was time to preach, Gerbole went to the pulpit. The girl who was praying alone came to him, crying. She got close to his ear and said, "Tell the assembly to be in prayer." She spoke to the assembly what the Lord had revealed to her:

> An army of evil spirits came from the deep to disturb the conference. When they reached in the air where we are, their goal could not be fulfilled, because of God's protection that was in place. Therefore, they went back to increase their force and returned with many times their original number. But when the angel of God stretched his rod, the air was filled with fire, and the demons, who came from one direction, dispersed in many directions and disappeared. They came the third time from all four directions, filling the sky. When they reached in the air over us, God gave a command, and they became ashes that fell down to earth. Why should I pray? God has already fought the necessary battle for this conference.

The girl also pointed out the weakness of the church in not being prepared in prayer and not trusting God's faithfulness. At that point, amazed by what God had done, the prophet stood at the podium and shed tears. The assembly was also in tears, marveling at God's faithfulness and protection.

After that, the assembly felt released and free. Evil spirits shrieked and the Holy Spirit came down with power, and the meeting place shook. Many sick people were healed miraculously. Healing came even to some choir members and ministers.

The assembly became free from all evil spirits and illnesses. Two convicted felons who had escaped from prison saw this gathering while on their way into hiding. They decided to stop by, although it was not known why they did that. The Scripture portion the preacher read was "It is hard for you to kick against the goads" (Acts 9:5 NKJV), and the topic of the sermon was "It Will Be Worse for You."

The felons listened to the preaching, which had references throughout from the Bible. The central message was about the damage done to oneself by opposing God's plan. But what registered in their minds was the topic: "It Will Be Worse for You." They said to themselves, "This guy from the city knows that we have escaped from prison. We will stop him before he reports us." So they planned to attack him on his way home and waited for him, hidden down by the river.

After Prophet Gerbole finished his ministry, he started his return trip to Ashi by mule, escorted by two deacons. They passed through the forest of wild coffee trees, descended into the valley, and reached the river. The mule refused to cross the river. All means were tried, but it refused and in fact began to backtrack.

Even when Gerbole dismounted and tried to pull it, the mule did not change its mind. Gerbole said, "Lord, what did I do wrong? I am not like Balaam who traveled for rebellion. I traveled to serve. What did I do wrong?"

Meanwhile, the two felons who escaped from prison and felt the sermon was directed against them came out of the forest to avenge themselves. Both of them approached the travelers with their sticks at the ready. However, before they were able to use their sticks, the prophet used his weapon, which is the Word of God. When he said, "He who is with us is greater than he who is with you," one of them threw his stick away and sat down, as he could not keep his balance. This was how Gerbole related to us what happened next:

> As we heard from the felons themselves, two officers who were visible to them but not to us came and arrested them. The felons said, "You had us caught by hiding these two soldiers here, right?" They marched ahead of us, saying, "Okay, okay!" as if they were being driven by someone. Even if the felons waited for us in hiding, God waited for them in hiding. The soldiers protecting us were visible to them, and truly, it was to them that they needed to be visible, because to us, our faith was our seeing.
>
> After that, the mule obediently crossed the river while the felons were driven ahead of us to Ashi town. We followed them to see the end of this drama. The angels driving the felons took

> them to the police station and made them be seen by the police. Because the police could not see the heavenly officers, they thought the escapees came to surrender willingly and quickly took them into custody. Just like Peter followed what was happening to Jesus from afar, our surveillance from a distance was finished, and the two deacons who escorted me were amazed. Finally, we exchanged our good-byes and the deacons headed back home with the mule. And I went to the home of believers where I was staying. I was amazed for a long time by what happened and rejoiced about the Lord's protection.

There is more to add before we drift away from the subject about the Lord's protection. In this case, the person who related the story to us was the husband of Adanech's sister (Adanech is Prophet Gerbole's wife).

One time when I was returning from Illubabor, and Gerbole was on his way home to Gida from Addis Ababa, we met in Nekemte. After reserving our hotel rooms, we stepped out to have dinner. While we were walking, he stopped suddenly. I said, "What happened to you?"

He said, "Let us go back. The Lord has said to go back." We returned and spent the night on empty stomachs. From the report we received in the morning, it was necessary that we spend the night without food. We heard that in the area we had planned to go that evening, people fought and killed each other, and many others who were not involved were also hurt.

In that same year, we met again in Nekemte. As Gerbole continued on to Addis Ababa, he bought his ticket, and I saw him off as he boarded his bus. He got off the moving bus and came back as I was leaving the terminal. I asked him what happened. He said, "The Lord told me to get off." He tore up the ticket, even though it was difficult to get a ticket and he had no money to buy another one. If it were another person, he would have sold it very easily for a much higher price. But Gerbole did not want to sell the ticket for a trip of which God did not approve, with all its consequences. The bus he was going to travel on left Nekemte. After it had traveled sixty kilometers, however, it fell into a ravine between Sire and Bako. The information reached Nekemte at ten o'clock, and it was reported in the news that forty-three of the sixty-five passengers died in the accident.

The following day, Gerbole entered the bus terminal without any money to buy his ticket but just trusting the Lord, who had saved him the previous day by telling him to get off the bus. While he was pacing back and forth, waiting for God to do what He had to do, he saw a certain lady waving from among a crowd of people and calling, "Gerbole! Gerbole! Come here!" She greeted him, breathing fast, and asked, "Where are you going?"

He answered, "Addis Ababa."

"Have you bought your ticket?"

He replied, "No, I have not."

And then she said, "Do not buy one. I bought a ticket to travel directly from Dembi Dollo to Addis Ababa, but now I am not continuing because I have something to do here. Here is the ticket. Get on this bus quickly."

In this way, she got him swiftly onto a bus that was full and about to move out of the terminal. And as for me, I had run out of money, as I had stayed a day longer with Gerbole. As he was getting into the bus, I asked him what I should do. He said, "Stand here and wait. God will come for you." He left and I started waiting for God, as he told me.

I had not waited for God before and did not have the experience in this field. Since the direction He would be coming from was not known, I was looking here and there. Then, a certain person I knew from my area in Illubabor saw me from afar and came toward me. After exchanging greetings. he said, "It is good that I met you. What would I have done if I had not met you? I was looking for someone who is familiar with the city. I came for my driver's license. You will stay with me today, and we can go home together tomorrow when we are done with it."

He asked me this as a favor, and we finished his business that same day. He said, "From now on, you stay here at my expense." He paid for my hotel and bus ticket and gave me one hundred birr. The following day I traveled home.

Another experience is the ministry challenge that Gerbole faced in one village. The believers in that particular village had invited him repeatedly to minister to them. When such invitations came, he would always ask, "Lord, is it your will that I should go? Is there something you want to do there?"

Since he did not get an answer to his question, he did not go to this village to minister. But at a time when they were not expecting him and when the thought was completely out of his mind, the Spirit of the Lord told him to go to that church.

Gerbole took with him Teacher Tilahun from Gida. He waited for their regular day of gathering and walked into the service. After exchanging greetings with the leaders, he said to them, "It is now that the Lord gave me a message for you. Tilahun will lead, and I will preach." In this way, he told them the reason for his coming.

One of the members of the leadership team got up and said, "You did not come when we invited you. You should serve when we want and not when you want. Nobody knows about your life, and you simply roam around, and you do that for sex and not for ministry. In fact, you will not stand on our pulpit." He pushed Gerbole away from the platform.

The owner of the house where the meeting was being held stood up and added to the ideas of the first person. She said, "Gerbole will not minister. The life of a minister who did not show up when we needed him is suspect. He has moral issues."

After listening to both, Gerbole said, "You do not know me. It is the Lord who knows me. If you do not want me to minister to you, okay. Let it pass you." As he retreated, he said to the man, "God says this to you: 'You will not stand on the podium you are standing on today. This is your last time.'"

Gerbole's father-in-law, who was there at the time, knew the life of Gerbole and that what spoke through him never missed its mark. He begged Gerbole, saying, "Please do not curse them, because if you do, all the people will be cursed."

"I did not curse them, but because it is written, 'Woe to those who call good, evil and evil, good,' it is they who brought a curse upon themselves," responded Gerbole, and he and his partner returned from where they'd come.

The person who was told that it would be his last time on the podium became totally paralyzed immediately and died after a week. The lady who made additional comments lost a large flock of sheep and goats on which she depended, as they became sick and died.

CHAPTER 12

THE INTERVENTION OF GOD

> Elijah was a man just like us. He prayed earnestly that it would not rain, and it did not rain on the land for three and half years. Again he prayed and the heavens gave rain, and the earth produced its crops.
>
> —James 5:17–18

God is close especially to those who strive for truth. He is close to those who are close to Him. They become the manifestation of His glory and His servants. Because Moses was close to God, ten plagues happened in Egypt during the time of his leadership. Also, the sea parted, water gushed out of rocks, and powerful kings were defeated. One person who could be an example of being close to God is Prophet Gerbole. What we learn from his life is that God can intervene in every circumstance and do things, and He can use us without any limits when we come close to Him. It is like what Jesus said about doing more than He did if we believe.

In the summer of 2009, Prophet Gerbole and his wife, Adanech, had traveled to Dila University for the graduation of

Adanech's brother. They started from Addis Ababa and descended to the Rift Valley and continued their long journey. At Modjo, they turned ninety degrees right and passed through Meki, Ziway, Shashemene, and Awassa. Even after they traversed the hot areas of the lowlands and reached the higher elevation, the temperature was hot, in spite of the fact that it was the rainy season. The usual green hue of the landscape of Dila and its environs was not there at that time.

It had not rained for months, although it was the season when the corn crop would normally have been at a stage when the stalks began to develop. In fact, there was no sign of the rainy season or any trace of clouds in the sky. The crops of the few farmers here and there who went ahead and planted—following the season in spite of the drought—had dried up or wilted. Dila and its surroundings, which would normally be adorned by flowering banana trees and other crops to the delight of onlookers, was without its verdant cloak and was completely dry. The trees had lost their leaves, and the ground was bare. It was in this condition that Dila University welcomed parents of its graduating students and guests.

To us Ethiopians, who live in an environment that relies heavily on the consistency of the seasons, it is normal that the delay of the rainy season would attract our attention. The guests in Dila must have been shocked to find the dry and sunny climate in the middle of what was supposed to be the rainy season. But there were only two from among the guests who thought of solutions for the problem. As a result of the intense heat, they could not get any sleep the whole night in their hotel room. The drought condition they observed during the day, coupled with the disturbing heat they were experiencing by night, convinced them that a solution must be found. Gerbole and Adanech prayed this short prayer to the Lord, who was near during the night: "Please give rain tomorrow after the end of the graduation ceremony."

Right after the graduation program, as people went back to where they came from, the windows of heaven were opened, and it rained. The ground that had cracked and opened its mouth was soaked, and the rainy season continued.

"The Lord was with Samuel as he grew up, and he let none of his words fall to the ground" (1 Sam. 3:19).

The work of God is a job of battling with the ruler of this world, Satan, and his demons. Wherever the gospel reaches, it dislodges evil, clears the forest, and conquers the land. It has never come across completely open space. That is why it was said, "The people living in darkness have seen a great light" (Matt. 4:16). If people are not in the light, they are in darkness, which means darkness has to be removed for the light to be present. God said, "Let there be light," and there was light" (Gen. 1:3). The ministry of the gospel is a service to nurture the life of light and the act of saying let there be light in the midst of darkness. And this, of course, causes conflict with the ruler of this world, as it involves demolishing one kingdom and establishing another kingdom in its place. The church demolishes the kingdom of the Enemy and builds the kingdom of God.

In spite of the fact that there have been challenges in the ministry of the prophet of demolishing the kingdom of the Enemy, just as for any other minister, the hand of God has done mighty things, because it has been declared that "the gates of hell shall not prevail against the church." We will selectively present some of the things God has done in this regard for His honor and glory.

First, Evangelist Amru Hundesa from Wanki spoke:

> In 1993, Prophet Gerbole ministered twice in Wanki, Western Wollega. On his first visit, he declared that the big tree that was being used for demonic worship was the reason that the community drifted away from God and became destitute. He said from that time on, the tree would not be worshipped and that the people would turn to God. Not long after that, the tree dried up and fell, and the heart of the people became open to the gospel. The light shone in the darkness, and a big church was established at that location.
>
> When Gerbole ministered the second time, there was a chairman of the community who did not like the church and was a persecutor. He came with armed guards to the home where the meeting was being held, with the purpose of taking Gerbole into custody. But he could not arrest Gerbole, who was right in front of him. He took others and detained them. Nobody showed Gerbole the home of the chairman, but he stretched his hand and rebuked the obstacle to the gospel. When Gerbole was leaving the area

> after the close of his ministry, the children of the chairman set their house on fire, and it burned down. His entire herd of cattle was decimated by a lightning strike. One of his sons developed a mental sickness. The chairman understood that he was fighting with God and resigned his position. When he was handing over the office to his successor, he said, "Let alone going to them and taking steps against these *Pentes*, do not touch them, even if they come here." Eventually God helped that person to repent and become a worshipper after he wrote a letter to the church asking for forgiveness.

Evangelist Jiregna Ayana from Guliso added his testimony:

> At the 1995 conference in Guliso, there was a wonderful visitation of God. Among the things that took place, the one that amazed both believers and the town was the miracle that happened to the HIV/AIDS patient Desse Mamo. She was not able to eat or drink and was brought to the conference on a stretcher and placed away from the gathering. The prophet walked to the place where she was lying down and said, "In the name of the Lord Jesus, get up. Carry what you are lying on and go."
>
> She was immediately healed and stood up. Fully healthy again, she rolled up her bedding,

went to the platform, and testified how God touched her. She reached home after walking for about twenty-five minutes. After that, the woman was freed from waiting for the time of her death and lived in peace and health.

In the course of the same conference, the prophet was one time returning to the place where he was staying when a man opposed to the gospel called out "Gerbole" twice by mimicking a woman's voice to make fun of him. When Gerbole turned around, thinking that a woman was calling him, he saw that it was a man. The voice of the man remained like that of a woman, and his wife died a month later. He himself became crazy and walked the streets of the town naked for a long time.

Pastor Nigussa Desalegn offered the following:

In December 1993, a colleague and I were ministering in Kiremu when we were thrust into a difficult situation as a result of the trap that the Devil and evil people had set up against us. But God sent Prophet Gerbole to us. Through God's leading, he came directly from Gedo to where we were and saved our lives by receiving the evil cup that was prepared for us. At another time, we traveled together from Hareto by foot and by raft through the swampy region and reached Abay

> Chomen. One thing that surprised me during the service was how he handled screaming people who were demon-possessed. He said to them, "This is the time when we listen to the Word of God. Until then you go assemble and wait under the pine tree (*zigba*). We will meet when the time set aside for you comes."
>
> After he said that, all the demon-possessed people who were shouting moved under the tree without anyone forcing or carrying them. When he was done with the service, he said to them, "Now is your time; come out!" All the demons came out shrieking.

On one occasion when Gerbole and I were ministering in Kiremu, nothing significant happened for about half of the day. Heaven was closed, and we understood that the power and challenge of the Enemy was standing against us. Prophet Gerbole understood in the Spirit that someone was hiding in the eucalyptus forest at the back and casting a spell over the gathering. He prayed repeatedly that this person would turn away from his evil ways. He felt that if he went ahead and told the gathering, it would cause physical and religious conflict and rob them of spiritual victory. And so he simply began to demolish this work of evil through prayer. Then the situation changed. And finally, he said in general terms, "In a few days they will pick up from under a tree the body of the person whom the devil used to stand against this assembly."

That same week, that person was found dead under a tree with his stomach distended. He used to be a known worker of the kingdom of darkness, but in this campaign, he could not return to his home. Just as he used to do witchcraft under a tree, he fell and remained under a tree. He should have quickly repented and accepted the lordship of the Messiah as soon as his stomach began to distend. He knew he was defeated but lived in darkness and went to eternal darkness with his eyes open.

CHAPTER 13

The Sojourn in Burayu

Prophet Gerbole changed the location of his family home many times as his ministry continued to expand. The apostle Paul had undertaken many long and important missionary journeys during his ministry. At first, he would just commend them to the Lord, and then he began to organize them as churches. Later, during the years when he was in Rome, he built the churches through his epistles. Likewise Prophet Gerbole's ministry also gradually decreased in terms of long trips and especially after he moved to Burayu, a suburb of Addis Ababa, in 2010. After that, he gave phone service to many around the world, counseling and praying for them. People called from the United States, Canada, Europe, and Australia and shared their burdens. The phone calls stopped only when the cell phones were being charged.

Here is how Prophet Gerbole describes his ministry:

> One day I felt tired after ministering over the phone the whole day, and I lay down to rest. Right as I was dozing off, someone came and said, "Get up, get up," and woke me. However,

there was no one there when I got up and looked around the house. Since the person had awakened me by actually holding my shoulder and shaking me—and it was not in my dreams—I thought it was a family member.

But the hand that shook me and the person who said, 'Wake up; someone is waiting for you,' was not around. I got up and waited for the person who was looking for me. Then it dawned on me that I'd been giving service through the phone, so I turned on my cell phone, and in less than two minutes, it rang. Parents were calling; their son was seriously sick in America. They said, "Our son is sick, and we are in a hurry to take him to the hospital. We called you so that you would pray for God's intervention."

We then prayed together, with the parents laying their hands on their son by faith. The boy opened his eyes right away, his sickness subsided, and he started to talk. They abandoned the plan to go to the hospital. And I said, "Lord, forgive me"—I realized that I had slept while there were people in need. I repented. The Lord said to me, "Why are you resting when I am not? I will be with you and give you more strength when you get tired. Many will be released from their stress through you."

After that, I never turned off the phone unless it was charging or I had a prayer time. I did not

> turn off the phone just to take a rest when I was tired. Even when I did, I kept listening to the Lord, just in case there was something for which I was needed.

The Lord has solved many people's problems during these two years of phone ministry. Both men and women have told me everything in their hearts, openly, just as they would pour out their secrets to God. I have kept their secrets faithfully, and God has met their needs in amazing ways. The prayer requests I've received by phone are in regard to health, marriage, and spiritual problems. When it comes to health and sickness issues, the highest number of requests have come from developed countries in the West. In spite of the number of doctors, the sophistication of the equipment, and the effectiveness of the drugs, the sickness is sometimes not identified. In such cases, God uses illness as a way to pin down people who do not respond to His gentle promptings.

It is appropriate here to quote Job 22:22–28.

> Accept instruction from his mouth and lay up his words in your heart. If you return to the Almighty, you will be restored: If you remove wickedness far from your tent and assign your nuggets to the dust, your gold of Ophir to the rocks in the ravines then the Almighty will be your gold the choicest silver for you. Surely then you will find delight in the Almighty and will lift your face to God. You will pray to him, and he will hear you, and you will fulfill your vows.

> What you decide on will happen, and light will shine on your ways.

With regard to marriage, both married and unmarried people have questions. The common issues between husbands and wives are with regard to not being faithful to each other, "he/she left me" accusations, arguments, misunderstandings, and fights. Most of the time, the person with whom I get in touch is the victim. I counsel the person to get closer to God in the situation he/she is in. There are two reasons for this approach. The first one is that God can intervene and adjust their marriage, and second, so that they do not lose the eternal that goes beyond marriage. Just like King Saul's uncle said that Saul's father was more concerned for his son than the lost donkeys, it is better to enter heaven with just one eye. The main purpose is to protect the spiritual life of the person.

It is expected that the love of persons who have been married for a long time will increase as they pass through life's ups and downs. However, contrary to this expectation, there are times when couples grow apart, to the point where they separate. There also are couples who, after beginning in poverty, become well-to-do by God's blessings, look down on each other, and say, "He/she does not measure up to me." As a result, they end up making wrong choices.

Not having children is another problem of marriage. A couple should never forget the covenant into which they have entered. The problem of many Christian husbands and wives is forgetting their covenant. The covenant that states "In times of difficulty and times of need" does not apply only to finances; it should be remembered when there is bareness. The marriage covenant is not negotiable, whether a couple is able to have children or not. Instead of blaming one another as the cause for not having children and weakening the bond of the covenant, they should come before the Lord in unity, and it would be possible to have children. We have seen countless barren couples bear children after being prayed for.

The problems of singles are not easy either. The first problem is confusion in making choices—"Who shall I marry?"—as the candidates could be many. At that point the key is to rely wholly on the Lord and ask for guidance. To follow one's desire and decide on the basis of external things, like wealth and beauty, does not help to establish a long-lasting marriage. In addition to loss and disappointment, such a marriage will not go far.

"A wife of noble character who can find?" (Proverbs 31:10).

God is able to find you one; seek His face. I have met those, especially many sisters, who have missed marriage as a result of not accepting the partner God has given. Instead of closing their eyes and waiting for God, they open their eyes and search for the husbands they want. Even when God tells them, 'This is the one for you,' they do not hear, because they are in the midst of a serious hunt. They wake up after their age has advanced, having lost the one they were pursuing because it was not of God, as well as the one He prepared because of timing. They lose on both counts and begin to desperately search for husbands.

Singles, allow God to choose for you, as He does not make mistakes. It has been said, "I know the plans I have for you … plans to give you hope and a future" (Jer. 29:11). Have faith in the Lord to save our souls. He is trustworthy to take care of the other things.

There are also problems that come out of the period of engagement. While the couple may meet according to God's will, it is possible that the relationship might end as a result of a long engagement that produces familiarity, and they may become tired of each other, or others may intervene. Such things leave a lifelong loss and scar.

Another thing I experience through this phone ministry is the weakening of spiritual life. This spiritual weakness and coldness is caused by time constraints, limiting one's investment in studying the Word of God and participation in spiritual activities. Many call me, especially from overseas, about the weakness of their spiritual lives.

Irrespective of where we live, our fellowship with God should not change. If we do not have time for prayer, the Word, and fellowship with saints, the warmth that is in us will slowly cool down and eventually disappear. We have to feed and keep the fire burning before it goes out.

"I remind you to fan into flame the gift of God, which is in you through the laying on of my hands" (2 Timothy 1:6).

This applies to all believers. The spirit within us must be aroused, ignited, and continue to grow, for without this, our spiritual life becomes empty and remains only ritualistic and religious. The Word of God advises us to pray in the Spirit, sing in the Spirit, and understand the Word in the Spirit. The fact that the Lord said, "I came that you might have life and have it abundantly," indicates that the life of faith keeps on growing and multiplying. How do we get transformed unless life is ignited by the Holy Spirit? What God expects from us is not just to be the inheritors of His kingdom but also to be transformed into the likeness of His Son and beyond.

"So I say, live by the Spirit, and you will not gratify the desires of the sinful nature. For the sinful nature desires what is contrary to the Spirit, and the Spirit what is contrary to the sinful nature. They are in conflict with each other" (Galatians 5:16–17).

Unless we are strong in the Spirit, the flesh becomes the ruler over our Christian life, and a Christian life under the control of the flesh will only bear bad fruit. Since life is manifested through the fruit we bear, it takes a spiritual life to produce fruits of the Spirit.

Another area that the Lord has shown me is to minister in a regular church service. My phone-counseling ministry will be for a limited time, except for those who live far away. We are preparing in prayer and other ways to construct a building soon and start a regular church service on the plot given to us in the western part of Addis Ababa, on the border of Kolfe-Keranio in Burayu zone. It is my belief that people will receive God's blessings through that ministry.

CHAPTER 14

THE CHILDREN

Prophet Gerbole does not minister only to people outside his home, but he also serves his family and gives them adequate time. Once, when members of the family were all together, he said to his children, "Each of you think about anything you want and ask me any question you might have."

"What kind of question?" they asked.

"Anything you want; it could be about money or some other thing," he replied.

The first child, Kenna, took the first opportunity, because she had a project that was not finished. She had started to make a bedcover and had done half of it when she ran out of thread. She said, "I need 180 birr to buy the thread."

Next, the mother said, "The *teff* supply is finished. I need money to buy *teff* and for my pocket as well."

Following that, all of them presented questions that were in their hearts. The father then said, "Are you done?" All of them replied, "Yes, we have finished."

The head of the house asked this question not because he had the capability to answer each one according to their questions but to give him a chance to listen to their problems, just as he ministered to other people. His idea was that if God helps him to solve other people's problems, He could also do it in Gerbole's family. He reasoned, "If God is ready to help them, why don't I collect their requests and present them to Him by faith?"

The family members waited for him to dip his hand into his pocket. Instead, Gerbole stepped out of the house, broke branches off a eucalyptus tree, and picked off the leaves. He then arranged them like dollar bills and returned to the assembled family.

"Here is the money you wanted," Gerbole said, and he gave his wife what she had asked to buy *teff* and for personal expenses and then to Kenna for buying thread for the bedcover project. He counted the right amount, according to their requests, and extended his hand for them to receive it.

Adanech rose up respectfully and, without hesitation, accepted the leaves she was given. The children murmured, "Dad, we asked for money, not for leaves. Are you joking like a child?"

They exchanged glances in confusion. The mother intervened and counseled them, saying, "Do what he tells you to do. Accept it as if it is money, and do not despise it because it is a leaf."

Each person accepted exactly what he/she asked for in white eucalyptus leaves. The house was filled with silence and the aroma of eucalyptus.

After Gerbole was done with the distribution, he said, "Today God will lead you into a new experience. Adi, please lead in a prayer of gratitude for what happened, in which God gave you according to your request."

There was a knock on the door while all were standing and Adi was leading in prayer. But since the prayer of thanksgiving is a big sacrifice that is presented to God and should not be stopped, Adi continued calmly and stopped when she was finished. The two persons outside the door had stopped knocking when they realized that prayer was going on. When the prayer was finished, the door was opened for them, and actually there were three, including their guide.

While the guide stayed outside, the two persons entered the house and greeted the family. They were new people who had come from far and were not known to Gerbole and his family or their neighbors. When the prophet stepped out of the house to pick the eucalyptus leaves, he had prayed, "Please Lord, do not embarrass me in front of these children. Send a response that flies like an arrow."

These people were sent and already were on the road before he prayed that prayer. This means that we say some of our prayers when the answer is already on the way. This kind of prayer could be called the visitation of God. It is the act of God to awaken us to what is happening by placing in our hearts the desire to seek and to do.

Therefore, since the people God sent for this visitation and to amaze that household were already on the way, the prophet's act of faith became the transfer of blessings. When the two guests were invited to come in and sit down, they said, while still standing, "We were sent here, and please accept the message."

The family asked, "What is your message?" They said, "We have brought a gift," as they looked for something in which to put their bundles of money. They were given a flat basket, and they put the gift on the basket. Then the prophet testified to them what had taken place before their arrival, including the act of placing leaves, which were drying up then, in the hands of the children. He told them how their gifts had arrived in the midst of the family's faith-filled waiting and how he passed hope to the family through the miracle of sharing leaves. The guests rejoiced in the fact that they were at that place in perfect obedience to God, and they went their way after thanking God, in tears.

After the guests were sent off, the members of the family received money according to their request and the number of leaves in their possession. In other words, the leaves were exchanged for money. Gerbole took the rest of the money for his next ministry and traveled, leaving behind his family, who were renewed by a new level of faith and experience.

God can do new things that are outside our experience. Many times when we pray, we seem to give indications to God of how the prayer should be answered. But He is a great God and has tens of thousands of ways to answer our prayers. In Numbers 11:18–31, when God said, "Consecrate yourselves … you will eat meat … the Lord will give you meat," Moses had difficulty believing it. Considering the short duration and the size of the population, he could not believe that a whole "country" could be supplied with enough meat to go around.

What was difficult for Moses to understand was that God said He would give them meat. So he asked, "Would they have enough if flocks and herds were slaughtered for them? Would they have enough if all the fish in the sea were caught for them?" (Num. 11:22).

According to Moses' experience, the sources of meat are two—from flocks and herd on land or from the fish of the sea.

But the meat came from a source outside Moses' experience. Meat was found where there was neither herd nor flock to slaughter nor sea to catch fish. "A wind went out from the Lord," and the wind became the butcher. From where the people camped and where the tabernacle was in the center to a distance of one day's journey in each direction, meat hung in the air without any hooks at about the three-foot level. It was not meat that would satisfy them but meat from which they could not escape because of its bad odor that flooded their camp.

The faith and request of this family did not come from coveting but as a result of their obedience and their offering of praise, before the answer actually came. As a result, it entered their house carrying a heavenly bounty of joy.

Those children, born in the midst of hardship, did not continue to be that way. They grew up knowing and being familiar with the Lord. Kenna, the first of the six children, continued to speak words of faith, beginning from early childhood, not afraid to rely on the Lord. She had a life based on faith and a full heart on the closeness of the Lord. When she was a high school student, she became sick with typhoid and had to be admitted to the hospital in Nekemte, because she waited too long before getting treatment. She stayed there for two months and was unconscious, hanging between life and death. The mother and father had to take care of her, leaving the rest of their children at home. The mother never left her bedside, day and night, while the father was loaded with ministry. He served within the city of Nekemte and in the hospital itself and prayed for sick people. He also ministered to the nurses and workers' fellowships.

Kenna's doctor, who observed this, asked Gerbole, "Why do you pray for all these people, and you do not pray and heal your own daughter, who has been unconscious this long?"

Gerbole answered the question in a composed manner. "Doctor, you are a physician. When you get sick, do you examine and treat yourself, or do you seek the help of another physician?"

The doctor replied, "I do help myself with the health science I know, but I do not treat myself when I need medical attention. It is someone else who gives me treatment."

Gerbole responded, "Just like you, I do not serve myself with my gift. Just like any other man of God, I present my request to the Lord, who helps me. Since healing or not healing is His will, I will wait to see what will happen."

The doctor told him, "If your daughter stays like this, she will die. Do not hope for recovery and don't labor in vain."

"My daughter will not die, and even if she dies, she will go to be with the Lord. Therefore, if there is no hope in your treatment, we will take our daughter to the Lord," Gerbole said to the doctor.

"Yes, it would be good if you took her in good time," responded the doctor in a spirit of hopelessness.

Gerbole hastened to his daughter's hospital room. He looked at the faces of the mother and other close relatives who were huddled around the bed of the unconscious daughter. Hopeless eyes, pregnant with sorrow, received him. He said, "Get up, and let us take her home."

Everybody understood that when a patient in the hospital was rushed home before he/she recovered, the chances of being healed were remote. Thinking that she was going to die, tears started rolling from eyes that could barely contain them. But the prophet, who was determined, picked up his daughter, along with the other men, and carried her out. The ladies followed, and that day they kept her in a motel. Gerbole repeatedly rebuked the spirit of death, saying, "Death you are not allowed to take this child. Go away from her."

And Kenna was released slowly from the sickness that controlled her. Step by step, she regained consciousness and was able to recognize everybody. She was able to drink some fluid after being on glucose for two months. The following day she was able to support herself on the seat of a car, and they reached home in Gida. Slowly, her wobbly walk disappeared, and the recuperating Kenna returned to school, carrying her notebooks. She was welcomed by all her friends and started to pursue her education.

The doctor who asked why Gerbole didn't heal his daughter while he healed others never knew that Jesus was treating patients and bringing them back from the brink of death. But one day, he got the chance to experience this firsthand when his sister was sick with a brain tumor. It became necessary for her to go abroad for treatment, but the cost was beyond their capability. The doctor remembered the intervention of God's power when man's power was not sufficient, as in Kenna's case. Remembering her father's prayer and faith, he searched for Gerbole and found him. Although the prophet did not remember him, the doctor reminded him by telling the story, and they were reintroduced to each other.

He told Gerbole about his sister in Addis Ababa who was on the verge of death. When Gerbole asked him, "What shall I do for her?" the doctor replied, "Pray for her."

Gerbole answered, "How can you be a messenger for another before you yourself are saved? Therefore, first you have to be saved." The doctor repented and accepted the Lord as his personal Savior.

Continuing their interaction, the prophet said, "You see, when a person comes to you for the first time, doesn't he give his name and get a card?"

"Yes," replied the doctor.

"Now you have your card to see Jesus. Together we will tell Him about your sister's sickness. He will examine and treat her. Please connect me with your sister by phone," said Gerbole.

The doctor called and connected Gerbole with his sister, and so Gerbole was at the Nekemte end of the line, and the sick lady and the physician Jesus were together at the Addis Ababa end. There was intermittent coughing, followed by a sudden spurt of blood from her mouth. The conversation ended.

"Your sister has been healed. Let her go and be examined by her doctor," Gerbole said. When she was examined, the tumor that needed a huge sum of money for treatment was not there. It had dissolved into the form of blood that came out of her mouth.

After Kenna completed her high school education, she and her sister Adisse studied nursing at the nursing college in Nekemte. Since it was necessary for Gerbole to pass through Nekemte for ministry to various places, he would stop by and talk to them as a father and friend. On one of his visits, he said, "Okay, my daughters, be strong in your studies and get jobs."

Kenna quickly said, "Father, the salary in this country will not be enough for me. I do not want to be employed here." She then asked, "How does one go to America?"

He answered, "What I have heard is, the opportunity to go to America is through DV—diversity visa—or marriage, but God could have other ways outside these as well."

Even if infrequently, Gerbole did not stop praying in the Spirit about the marriage of his daughters. One day Kenna told her father that she had a fiancé. He asked the questions that had to be raised and kept quiet. In due course, there was a wedding, and the ceremony was held at the Mekanissa Mekane Yesus (Lutheran) Church. Around that time, the young Fufa, Kenna's husband, was sitting down with his father-in-law, Gerbole, and talking. As they discussed his work and the country in which he lived, Fufa said, "Prophet, actually I was introduced to you by phone." When Gerbole asked him when and from where he had called, Fufa said, "A friend of mine called you from America and asked you to pray for him about marriage, and you did. And since I was with him, he introduced us to each other, and I said, 'Please pray for me also about marriage.'"

Gerbole asked his son-in-law, "What did I respond to you?"

Fufa said, "Your response was, 'I will not pray for you. God has prepared a marriage partner for you. Simply thank Him, and she will be revealed when the time comes.'"

"And how did you come to be the husband of my daughter?" Gerbole asked.

"I came from America, where I live, to visit my family and was introduced to Kenna in an unexpected way. After taking time to pray to discern God's will, we received confirmation and then notified our families," Fufa replied.

"I see! Actually, God arranged for all this to take place in the corner of my own house!" said Gerbole, looking intently at his daughter as a father would. He was amazed at the work of God and His ways.

Currently, Sister Kenna, along with her husband and first child, live in Las Vegas, Nevada. When she was ready to deliver her child, she called her father and said, "Dad, what I inherited from you is faith. Whatever happens, I would like to have my baby through normal birth and not by an operation."

When her labor began and she was admitted to hospital, they were prepared to operate, but she delivered without any problem.

The second child is Sister Addise. She also grew up exercising faith. Whenever she needed shoes or clothing, she did not ask her parents. She would lay her hands on her feet and say, "Oh shoes, come! These are blessed feet. Come for the sake of God's honor!" Then she would tell her parents, "Wait; they will come within a short time." And they did. Her special gift is to make peace between people. Currently, she is married and a mother.

Jonathan is the third child and the first boy and a college graduate. Martha is the beauty who was prayed over to stay in the womb during pregnancy until her father returned from a ministry trip. She was born in the tenth month of her mother's pregnancy.

One day, Martha gave her parents a hard time by saying, "I am hungry for honey and will not sleep unless you give it to me." The father rubbed her hands and prayed, saying, "Lord give her sleep and feed her honey in whatever way you want." She slept, and in the morning she expressed her joy, saying, "Even if you refused to give me honey, a white man who wore beautiful white clothing fed me honey."

When she was just eighteen, she said to her father, "Dad, I want to get married." But he said to her, "Since you have good results in your studies and could go to college and get your degree, first complete your education."

Her response was, "Ah, Father, as for me, I will not stop pursuing my education, even after marriage, but you know a husband is greater than a degree," which made him laugh. Since she was serious about what she shared with her father, and she and her partner were at a point where they were praying about it, their parents supported the decision. Currently, she is married and a student.

Out of six children, the only young ones who live at home are the daughter Israel and the son Yohannes. Even if most of the children have left home, the number of people in the house is not low because of the many guests they host. The amazing thing is that some of the guests are not those who stay for a few days and leave; they come for a month or more for rest. Just as Adanech, Gerbole's wife, said during their years of hardship, "Go and serve without any worry; the Lord is here for us," we see now that indeed the Lord was there for her children—those children that the father did not raise but the mother did, with the help of the Lord.

CHAPTER 15

Testimonies of Those Who Know Gerbole

The twelve tribes of Israel, who descended from God's friend Abraham, were liberated from slavery to become people of the covenant. The glory of God was revealed through them. They received the inheritance and had an entire tribe of priests available to them. Why was it that God said, "Whom shall I send? And who will go for us?" (Isaiah 6:8). What about the priests? And the chief priests? Why was there no one to send? And could there be a standard to which Gerbole measured up that most of us do not?

In addition to the ministries that God accomplished through his servant, the focus of this section is what people can learn from Gerbole's life and ministry. In what ways can he be an example and a role model for others? Since God does not differentiate among people, how is it that this person could talk face-to-face with God, and things happened so easily, according to the word of this servant?

Getting insight into this would help to answer the question people ask as to what is lacking in their relationships with God, that He has not used them as He has used this servant.

The time between 1974, when Gerbole gave his life to the Lord, and 2011, when this book was published in Amharic, was thirty-seven years. Is there anything that others have to say about him—people who know him, including those to whom he ministered and those who were his partners in ministry? Let us look at what some of them wrote:

Pastor Derese Geleta from Eastern Wollega

I began to know Prophet Gerbole in 1975, when he was just a young boy. He loved the Lord beyond his age. During those years of persecution, when we used to advise him to move cautiously, he would respond by saying, "I am not only ready to go to prison for the Lord. I am prepared to die." He passed through those difficult years without fear or holding back from serving the Lord.

I remember in 1976, when believers from Ebentu were rounded up and imprisoned, he was not arrested. He felt bad for not being among them and went to the authorities and said, "Include me with them," but they chased him away. He is a brother with a pure heart who loves to share the problems of brothers and sisters. He is one who loves the Lord and serves Him; who has the anointing of the Holy Spirit; who loves all equally, not inclined to tribalism, not affected by tension or sorrow; and who does not like complaining. He is a man of love and faith. He is generous and steadfast in hardship, one who clearly knows his faith and ministry and understands God. What makes me wonder is why many start out well but are not faithful after a few years. They get caught up in something and so do not last long. Those who last long and finish the race are blessed. Prophet Gerbole has continued his journey without any disruptions in his relationships both with God and man and, as a result, has become an example to many of us. It is my wish that he will finish the race in this way.

Pastor Getachew Tessema from Dire Dawa

Both the Old and the New Testaments are summarized by this verse:

"Love the Lord your God with all your heart, and with all your soul and with all your mind. This is the first commandment. And the second is like it. Love your neighbor as yourself. All the Law and Prophets hang on these two commandments" (Matt. 22:37–40).

In as much as the Bible is the foundation of our faith, and the summary is to love God above all and to love our friends as ourselves, we see by Gerbole's life that he has love for God and people. Gerbole reveals in action that he has love and a place for all—big and small, mentally deranged and healthy. He shares from the little he has. This person is like the bird that deprives herself and carries food in her mouth to her nest to feed her chicks. He shares with people even when his family is in need. He takes off his clothing and gives it to others in need.

Since love is the foundation of everything, and it is stated that if a person claims that he loves God without loving his brother, he would not be telling the truth, it is sufficient to look at the love in Gerbole's life to know who he is. The life of this person teaches us that we are liars if we are called Christians, pastors, or apostles but our lives are empty of love. I think he is a person God placed among us as a standard to measure us by.

Also, Gerbole's faith in God is strong. To him, God is near. He has no doubt that God would do whatever comes out of his mouth. He believes that God will do what he utters, directly relying on God, even without kneeling.

Just as it was said, "As the Lord, the God of Israel, lives, whom I serve, there will be neither dew nor rain in the next few years except at my word" (1 Kings 17:1), so results are seen from the word of Gerbole's mouth. Since God is with him and speaking to him, he believes that it will come to pass. This happens because he gave his life fully to God. He was tested and passed. He is not his own; he is God's bow and arrow, living a life prepared to plant and pull up. In addition, the words of his mouth do not conflict with God's thoughts and will. Just like Caleb said, "We should go up and take possession of the land, for we can certainly do it" (Numbers 13:30). Since Gerbole speaks for the will and glory of God and in agreement with the Holy Spirit, it does not take long for God to honor his word.

Alemu Wakjira, PhD student

While the ministry of Prophet Gerbole is accompanied by big miracles, I have seen that he is an example to all of us in his attentiveness to God's voice and in following His guidance. When he is invited to preach, but God's plan is for him to pray, it does not take him long to shift to that. He does not follow human programs and appointments.

Another element that makes him different is the fact that his life experience and prayer are based on faith. Among miracles performed by faith, I would like to mention the one that happened in 1999 at a conference at the Nejo Full Gospel Church. While the conference was in progress, a heavy rain approached, with thunder and lightning and even it began to sprinkle. It was unthinkable to stop the conference at that point. The prophet ministered, and the Lord's power was manifested, and he said this: "You, rain, we need this time. For the time being, pass by and rain somewhere else. You will rain here some other time." And the rain passed over slowly with its heavy load and started to come down some distance away. In this way, I have seen him stop rain that had already started. I praise the Lord for this gift of grace.

Pastor Mesele Tadesse from Shambu

Prophet Gerbole has a big role in my life. One day when I was a young boy, I was plowing in the field with oxen when he came to me and said, "Now it is enough for you. From this point on, you will plow the gospel field."

In this way, he made me make a final decision about the call to ministry with which I was struggling. In addition, he is loved by many brothers and sisters, and he is a messenger of God to those who are beneficiaries of miracles of healing and to all who know him. He is a person whose love, as a manifestation of the fruit of the Spirit, does not grow cold, and his behavior does not change. He does not get warm and cold based on circumstances and does not collude with evil people. He is always careful about his relationship with his God and lives according to God's Word. Therefore, we need to make him our example.

Prophet Yeshitila Mechi

I do not evaluate Prophet Gerbole on the basis of the miracles that happened in his ministry. True, ministry carries value because it is the fruit of one's life, but also it is possible to do miracles in the name of the Lord and not be recognized at the end. I measure Gerbole by who he is and by his Christian walk. Many people think he is simple-minded. True, he does not walk according to the wisdom of the world. In these matters, he is way behind. People evaluate him based on their own values. He is not simple-minded and, in fact, is superior to the smart ones. I would like to say two things about him:

I have seen that he is ready to pay any price and is determined for the things he believes.

Also, his ministry resembles that of the Old Testament. While the ministry of New Testament prophets focuses on building up people by speaking the Word in its prophetic sense, with corrections and adjustments, the prophets of the Old Testament are controversial, beginning from their character. For example, Hosea purchased a prostitute and married her. And when he got children, he gave them names that revealed the scary things that God was going to do.

Ezekiel was commanded to move from place to place with his things as a wanderer, to draw the attention of the public, to eat his food and drink water with fear, to sleep on one side for many days, and not to cry when his wife died.

Gerbole's ministry has similarity with the ministry of these prophets. He ministers through signs. One time, a lady lost a son, and Gerbole went to comfort her. After he sat there for some time, he took out a Walkman and started playing a song, just as the Spirit of the Lord had told him. For a time, the mourners who had packed the place were confused, but after some time, the Holy Spirit came upon the believers in the crowd and the mother, and they started to speak in tongues, to sing, and to praise. In fact, the mother, prompted by the Spirit, said, "My son went to be with the Lord. He did not lose." And she worshipped.

Another story that people testify about is the two springs that have sprung up as a result of Gerbole. One is at Degagole, his hiding place during the time of his persecution. The other one is in a dry field that was given to him when he got married. Today both springs are used for irrigation by his relatives.

One time when Gerbole was ministering at a place known as Kebetato, he gave a command to the assembly: "Pick up a stick." To demonstrate, he himself picked up one. "Take the stick home, and there will be health and wellness in your house. Touch your cattle and grain storage with the stick," he said.

People did as told, and the land was blessed in an amazing way. A minister who came from another church picked up the stick that Gerbole had used for demonstration and, by faith, put it at the entrance of his church where people would step on it, so that revival would come. Just as he believed, the move of the Holy Spirit was revealed more than before.

Pastor Habtamu

Pastor Habtamu, who has known Gerbole since 1991, has the following to say:

I had the opportunity to minister with him on numerous occasions and noted that physical healing seemed very frequent. It was at the conference in Beka that I saw something amazing happen and where the glory of God was revealed beyond what any human being could bear. Two deacons approached to wash Gerbole's feet. They competed between themselves to do it, but finally they agreed to share the responsibility by each washing one foot. While they were washing, the Holy Spirit came down upon them with mighty power. They spoke in tongues. And their lives and the lives and ministry of the choir and other leaders were changed.

What is learned from this is that the servant of God is a blessing to others, not because of what he does or speaks and the results that happen as a consequence of that but that God just uses the presence of his servant. The secret lies in the fact that God is present with him. If God is with us, we need not labor hard. He does things. I have seen that God's presence is with Gerbole in fullness.

Since Gerbole knows that God is with him and walks in that knowledge wherever he goes, he handles all spiritual ministries with full confidence. As an example, one time when he was ministering to the students at the Bako Agricultural College, Mitiku, a member of the fellowship committee, suffered from stomach illness and could no longer continue his education. He had decided to return home, but as a member of the fellowship, he had to first discharge his responsibility for the conference. But Prophet Gerbole told him that he was healed from his sickness. To prove his recovery, he went to the kitchen and drank two cups of coffee. Nothing happened to him. Even after that, he doubted the healing he received and asked the man of God, "How do I verify I am healed?"

As a college student, proof had significance for him. He was not convinced, even though Gerbole said to him, "Ask the Lord. He will tell you." Since Gerbole understood that he wanted a sign, he turned toward Mitiku and asked, "Which would you give to the Lord—your arms or your legs?"

"My legs," he answered.

"Which one—right or left?" Gerbole asked.

He said, "The left."

Then Gerbole touched his left leg with his finger, and right away the student slumped and fell to the ground. His friends said to him, "What happened to you? Get up." But he continued to moan. They asked, "What happened to your leg?" He said, "It is paralyzed. I can't feel anything. It is completely numb like a rock," and he continued to moan.

Many people gathered around him. "It would have been better for you not to have started this," his friends said to him. Finally, the prophet asked him, "Do you believe now that you have been healed?"

He said, "I believe, I believe." The moment Gerbole touched his leg again with his finger, Mitiku leaped up and stood, and his leg was restored to normal health. Mitiku gave his testimony of what God did for him when the program of the day started. He did not have to discontinue his studies and was able to complete his education

Another story about Bako is the serious malaria epidemic of 2004. The epidemic affected the whole area and many fell like leaves. Private medical professionals flocked there and set up clinics in big rented homes. But Gerbole, the man of God, said, "Spirit of death, leave this land." The epidemic stopped. The tents set up as clinics were dismantled. The homes that were turned into clinics were converted back to their original use. Just like the army of Ben-Hadad, which ran away overnight, death that had engulfed the whole area left the land.

I have learned from the prophet that above all else, we have to seek God. If we seek God, and He is with us, we will be a benefit to individuals, to churches, and to the nation. We note that the presence of ministers is essential to change the image of our country. We understand from this servant and his ministry that the hope of this land is founded on believers drawing nearer to God.

There is one thing that we need to properly understand: Gerbole was not born as a prophet but only lives as a prophet. He gives without reservation what is in his hand—the life God gave him for God to use in revealing Himself.

Before the apostles were called by the Lord, they had no idea that they would be sent as carriers of the message that would transform the eternal destiny of humanity. It was while they were going about their regular work that they received the great call. After that, they became the apostles of the Lamb, and the execution of the eternal plan of God landed on their hands, and they had faith in their caller. They lived apostleship and died apostleship. (*They were apostles in life and death.*) Ninety-nine percent became martyrs.

Today, it is hard to find a person who is faithful to his call. Those who live according to their call live for God and benefit people. People separated unto God are not limited to a spiritual ministry. They do many things that benefit the nation.

Elijah was a man like us, a prophet without blemish by spiritual standards. In addition, he stood against the house of Ahab, who had done injustice and played a national role in making the land dry and wet. Elijah proved the lordship and glory of God in a setting where demonic worship prevailed. He was concerned about who ascended to power and who was removed from power.

When Elisha replaced Elijah, he began his ministry by healing the water that made the land unproductive, making the lives of people better. We have been designated to be the salt of the earth in order to transform the life of our communities. What has the church or have we, who bear the responsibility, done for the community so that man, who is precious and for whom Christ died for his eternal glory, does not die like animals and end up in hell?

In his time, Elisha was a solution for old women without husbands and barren ones, as well as providing abundance in a time of famine. He was a man who repeatedly saved the land from Syrian raiders—modern-day terrorists. Since it is essential to apply the same standard, we are required to live a life that has the favor of God, so that our country can be free of hunger, sickness, and bloodshed, and our rulers can be God-fearing and productive. The authority of the church is huge.

When the Lord was on this earth in the flesh, He used to help all those in need. He fed the hungry and healed the sick. He raised the dead. But after the resurrection, we do not see Him as being available to all, except to go to the sea to find the disciples and feed them roasted fish. The reason is that He had given the authority to loosen and bind to the church. He handed over the responsibility to the church to handle anything that needs to be done for people. If the church does not do it, it will remain undone. Today, our land is languishing in poverty because the church has not carried out its mission. Beyond changing the political, economic, and social life of our country for the glory of God and benefit of our people, we should not forget that our country is also a white field ready to be harvested.

Why does Somalia remain destroyed? The reason is because there is no interceding church there. When I knew Mogadishu, there were no church buildings, other than the Catholic church built by the colonial rulers. When the Italians who lived there died off one by one, it became empty, and in the course of the war, the roof and doors were dismantled and sold. The fate of the church ended up like this, making the country a place where even a cross could not be seen. Since there is no intercessor, it became a furnace where the fire of war rages. The intervention of believers is crucial for the peace and prosperity of a nation.

The gospel changes individuals and the community, and ultimately, the country. What we mean by change is that a just and peaceful political administration, proper and ethical lifestyle, and an economic system free of misery and blessed should be created. Many of the earlier Western countries and Eastern nations, like South Korea, could be identified as proof that this can happen.

For example, Sweden today is among nations that have stable political and economic systems. Swedes used to be backward hunters until the eleventh century, when the message of the gospel reached the nation. The evangelist Boniface, who crossed over from England, found them worshipping trees. They worshipped a god called Thor on Thursdays by assembling under a tree. When Boniface preached the gospel to them, they said, "Our god is this tree."

When he said to them, "I will cut this tree, and you will know another true and only God," their response was, "You better be careful. Thor will kill you." However, he got their permission and cut down the tree. He did not die. He chopped the tree and split the logs and still did not die. He built a log cabin using the wood and invited them to come in and hear the message of the gospel. So the Swedes turned to the gospel of Christ when Thor could not save himself.

Then the people began to settle in various places and started living a peaceful life. They became an ethical and blessed people. They carried the gospel to Russia. The gospel made Norway, Russia, and Sweden what they really are, even if they have forgotten this fact today.

If we have the desire to see political, economic, social, and ethical change and transformation within our country, the agenda of reconciliation among our people through Christ should be our burden.

Then we are expected to present before the Lord the development and peace of the country in uninterrupted intercession. In order to speak into the life of the nation, the language and ability to speak what God can hear is found within the church. The only solution to the misery of Ethiopia lies in the groaning of believers and their personal contributions.

Prophet Gerbole prayed for the growth of the towns of Boji Dirmeji and Chekorsa along the Mendi road when he was there. At a time when medical services posed a major problem and people were frustrated by lack of roads, he said that the road would be asphalted in an unbelievable way, and other development activities would be carried out. It happened just as God said. The region changed and in fact, the county got to the point where it won a trophy. Just like the situation would have changed had there been ten righteous people in Sodom, the number of churches within Ethiopia is more than enough to change the situation in Ethiopia. The Chekorsa and Boji Dirmeji story is taken from the testimony of Pastor Aemiro Melkamu and Evangelist Abose Baes, who saw results from their diligent prayer for their community.

Habtamu Belete, journalist

Habtamu Belete traveled to Gida Ayana when he was the editor of the Amharic magazine Mil-at *and interviewed Gerbole for nine days. He summarized his observations as follows:*

I know Prophet Gerbole as a person because of his ministry. I have traveled as far as Horocho and met his family, brothers, and sisters. I realized that the prophet downplayed the ups and downs and difficulties he experienced in his life. Instead, he admired the wonders and miracles of God. One of the qualities this person is known for is his love. As far as I know and understand, I have seen in Gerbole the biblical kind of love that is pure and free of hypocrisy. We do not find this kind of love in the lives of many ministers. His love is accompanied by generosity. He is a practical person, because his love is combined by giving to those who are in difficulty and sharing himself.

At his home in Gida, there are rooms purposely prepared as places of rest for guests. Anyone who is headed to Gida and stops by his home will definitely get food and drink, adequate rest, and spiritual ministry by the time he leaves. This ministry is actually the responsibility of his strong wife, Mrs. Adanech Tolera. She handles all guests with a full smile and spirit of humility. The children, on their part, are diligent workers and serve the guests under the supervision of their mother. Most of the time, the house is used for prayer and sharing the Word of God. It is an oasis of rest for body and soul alike. It is where the sick get healed, the depressed get comforted, and the weak get strengthened before they return home.

On this journey to interview Gerbole, I had a chance to travel all the way to Horocho, where he grew up, and was able to hear and observe a lot—the field where he tended sheep and spent the day with Jesus who loved him, the cave at Degagole where he took refuge after being chased from his home, and the forest and rocky mountain where he prayed, hidden from the cadres of the Communist Party who were looking for him. Although that place was the habitat of venomous snakes and cobras, I was told that he and the other persecuted believers lived in peace in close proximity with the cobras. So that the snakes would not attack them, he spoke to them in the name of God, saying, "We are servants of the Lord of heaven and earth. Do not come to us." Since creation hears the voice of God and obeys, the people and cobras lived at peace with each other. While people persecuted the Lord who died for them, wild animals submitted to their rule by the power of His name.

The other thing I noted is that his brothers who persecuted him are now in the Lord. His perseverance has become the cause for the salvation of his family. As it is said, "Blessed is he who perseveres in persecution," today his entire family is blessed.

Evangelist Gemechu Tolera

Evangelist Gemechu Tolera is the son of Mr. Tolera of Beka and the brother of Adanech, wife of Gerbole. As such, he has experienced many ups and downs associated with the life and ministry of the prophet. Even though he has a lot to say, let us just look at a few comments:

Prophet Gerbole had to leave home at a tender age, before receiving the love of his family. In the outside world, persecution by the cadres of the military regime (*Derg*) awaited him. On top of that, there were not many believers in those days. The few believers were scattered all over the area, and it took from hours to days to get from one to the other.

Therefore, we can understand that his bearing hunger, nakedness, hatred, and injustice served as the foundation for the fruit that is seen during these later years. He would not have made it to the blessings of today had he not withstood that chapter of trouble and persecution. If we ask, "How did he persevere through that period?" we would have two answers. The first one is that the love of Christ is great. In as much as it is said, "Much water cannot quench love," a person into whose heart Christ has come would be strengthened to pay any price.

Second, the Lord Himself strengthens and makes one stand firm. God, who received little Samuel from his mother and raised him and made him accomplish great things, has raised many children by His love as father and mother and used them for His glory. It was the same for Gerbole as well.

Even after he rejoined the family and began to minister in Gojam, crossing the Blue Nile River, and even going to Addis Ababa, church leaders sent him back home, saying, "You are just a child. You go and help your family." Gerbole was not only pushed out by his family and the system, but he also was not liked by church leaders. The reasons he was given were "You will serve when you grow up" and "Your love has no borders; be reasonable."

Even at a later date, when they could no longer hide his ministry and had to forcibly accept him as their minister, he was given only three birr per month to live on. I remember a time when he and the person who was serving with him and whose wife was pregnant were returning home after receiving their pay. Gerbole gave his entire pay to the brother and came home empty-handed. Since he is a man of love, he does not understand hatred. In these long years of acquaintance, I have seen him giving in spite of the fact that he does not own much. God has not left him without something to give.

"Now he who supplies seed to the sower and bread for food will also supply and increase your store of seed and will enlarge the harvest of your righteousness" (2 Cor. 9:10).

Even when he has nothing to give, he will give the last thing he has or whatever belongs to the family.

I have seen many wonders and miracles happen through Gerbole's ministry, but let me share only three of them: Brother Angassu Hundessa, a resident of Kebele 01 (neighborhood) in Guder town, district of Toke Jutaye in Western Shoa, was at work stapling tax documents, gripping some pins with his teeth. Suddenly, one of the pins slipped into his throat. He suffered with great pain and depression for three months. Then, I attended a big spiritual conference organized by the Full Gospel Church in Guder.

On the second day of the conference, when Prophet Gerbole was ministering, he came to the pulpit and said, "There are those of you in this assembly who have been to clinics and hospitals and could not find any solution to your problems, and your sickness is not diagnosed. Now there is a solution for you from the Lord. The sickness of most of you will come out through coughing and vomiting." Angassu Hundessa, who carried the pin in his stomach for three months, was suddenly caught by a coughing attack and vomiting that reached down his gut. Something hard came out, covered with blood and pus, and in that was the pin. Today, this person is functioning well, although he no longer grips pins with his teeth.

The other story is about what happened in 2007 in Eastern Wollega, Ebentu district, and the town of Ande. The Fellowship of Christian Churches had organized a crusade, but Brother Gebre Lemi, one of the organizers, became seriously sick and slipped into a coma. Prophet Gerbole arrived at a time when the leaders were under great difficulty and pressure about the possible effect on the people and the results of the conference, should the brother die at that time. The Spirit of God led him to the home of the brother in a coma. He stood at the door of the sick brother and called out with a loud voice, "Oh, Gebre Lemi, get up!" Gebre Lemi heard the voice and immediately came out of the coma and stood up, healed and fully whole. He returned to his regular conference duties. Since he was a government employee, many of his colleagues came to see him and were amazed, and they accepted the Lord as their Savior. And beyond that, the authorities who were there and became believers said, "God is truly Lord, and the church should be supported." They then gave orders to give them a plot so they could build a place of worship.

Finally, I would like to speak about Prophet Gerbole's prayer of faith and the results. His ministry is based on the prayer of faith. One time he was ministering at a conference organized by the Full Gospel Church of Gori in Western Wollega. Since the gathering was huge and could not be held in the church building, it was decided that it should be moved to an open and wide field. The prophet stood on a temporarily built dirt platform and began to minister. However, since it was the dry and hot season, the heat was unbearable for the people who came from the churches of the surrounding area and filled the open field. Nevertheless, believing what could be done outside the realities of the season, the participants persevered in that situation by covering their heads, some with their clothing and others with branches of trees, and were fed from the heavenly table.

But for Prophet Gerbole, it was normal to depend on the God who works outside the realities of this world. He said to the crowd, "Let us pray that this heat of the sun be changed to cool air." He then commanded the people to rise, stretch their hands, and pray with him: "Oh God, Lord of Hosts, the people who came to hear your Word cannot withstand the heat of the sun. They have persisted in this condition because of their love for you. If it is your good will, we ask you with one accord and unity, in the name of the Lord Jesus Christ, let the air be cool, beginning from this minute."

In this way, he presented the assembly before God in prayer. As the outstretched hands came down, a cloud began to cover the sky from horizon to horizon, and the air started to cool down.

The assembly that witnessed this and saw the prayer answered instantly gave glory to God with an extended applause and loud shouts of joy. The work of God, who cooled down the hot weather, was seen by all the people of the area, as the miracle was not limited to the sky over those assembled. Many came to faith that day. It was indeed considered foolish not to come to the Lord, when God was so visible. Also, the presence of God increased the faith of many believers.

Nassir from Jimma

Nassir, who previously lived in Agaro and was one who witnessed the ministry of the prophet, explains the unique things he observed:

The Spirit of the Lord descended like I had never seen before. Children from the ages of seven to thirteen were filled by the Holy Spirit and intoxicated by joy in ways never experienced before. Many were healed from their sicknesses. Since the prophet stayed in my house, many called by phone or came in person to see him. One lady in particular, whose sister was seriously sick, called many times, asking for prayer. He listened to the Lord and said to her, "Your sister will die next week. Give her everything she wants, and prepare food she likes. Talk to her with joy and in the remaining time, say your good-byes secretly." It happened exactly as he said.

On the day he was scheduled to depart, many people gathered at the door of our house very early in the morning. They came to bid him farewell and give him gifts. Gerbole said to me, "As a result of the wonders and miracles that happened the last few days, people want to honor me instead of seeing the Lord. The Lord has said to me, 'Give freely what I gave you.'" As a result, Gerbole said, "Get me out of this town in secret." I took him out in a car and put him on a bus to Jimma.

Evangelist Seqeta Geleta

Evangelist Seqeta is the person who prayed for Gerbole back in 1974 when he was a sick boy and was carried into the church at Daregos. Later, they also lived together for some time. Seqeta has this to say about Gerbole:

I have known him for thirty-seven years, and his love for people and his faith and undiluted unity with God amazes me very much. Even though he led a life of many ups and downs, beginning from the time he came to know the Lord, he has become a model to many by standing firm in his faith. In as much as what God wants from us is that our light will grow in intensity from the time we begin until we finish, this person has always been very careful about his character and spiritual life, as I have known him from childhood to gray hair.

Evangelist Eshetu Hordofa

> *"Set apart for me ... for the work to which I have called them" (Acts 13:2).*

God calls ministers for the work of His kingdom. There are ups and downs as well as twists and turns that those who are called must negotiate to get to the work to which they are called. Ministers who are just beginners very much need the advice and prayers of those before them, in order to be fruitful for the rest of their lives. Evangelist Eshetu Hordofa was just a young boy called by God, living in Gidami before he established the International Gospel Emancipation Ministry.

The future race he would run existed only in God's thoughts, and neither he nor the church of which he was a part knew anything about it. So Prophet Gerbole was sent to Gidami to tell him that God had plans to raise him up and that a big heavenly call has been sent to him. Therefore, when the prophet reached Gidami, he spoke to the young boy, whom he had not seen before.

Evangelist Eshetu says:

Prophet Gerbole told me that he came because the Lord said, "Go and grab his hand and bring him out." He then told me the details of my life history. I came out of there and slowly entered into this international ministry, just as he said.

First, what amazes me is how clearly he hears God. The manner in which he hears God is very unusual. He receives messages and passes them on to the concerned people, even when he is the midst of greeting others. In addition to his spiritual ears being instruments for finding solutions to people's problems, he also corrects those who tell him lies about their lives and brings them back to the truth.

The second good thing is that he is a person who lives for others. He gives himself to others on top of his ministry and gifts. He gives his money, clothing, heart, and time. He lives a sacrificial life for others.

Another good thing I have seen in him is that he never tires of ministering. He will be at the podium the whole day, ministering, and then spend the entire night in prayer. He meets and talks to people and advises them. His prayer is more than presenting the problems of people to God. It is by longing to see the face of the Lord that he approaches the throne of righteousness. I have seen that God uses him in a very special way. I have seen him call people he did not know by their correct names. This person has many spiritual assets that can be examples for us.

Evangelist Solomon Benti

This evangelist, who says, "Prophet Gerbole is a preacher and announcer of love and compassion," makes the following three observations about the minister:

Gerbole is a servant of God, whom He uses in powerful ways. I have heard stories told and seen things that happened in an amazing way, including those that occurred where we ministered together.

We are close at the family level, so I know that this minister is a good person and an example to all of us and one who lives a blessed life.

And he loves all people equally. He serves all without comparing ministry and personal benefits or city and countryside but just by asking the will of his Lord.

Obsse Mizanu

I have experienced repeated problems with bearing children. I gave birth to my first child at seven months, and she died after four months. I then conceived a second time, but the baby died when I was in labor, and I was delivered by an operation. While we were living in sorrow and with broken hearts because we did not get children, who are blessings of married life, Prophet Gerbole came to my office for his own purpose. I told him that I had something that made me very sad and asked him to pray for me. After he prayed over my chair, he said, "You will conceive after one month. Let me know when you are three months pregnant." Then he left.

As he said, I conceived after one month. On the fourth month, he came to my office and prayed for me. He did it again on the seventh month. When I was due to deliver and was admitted to hospital, he came without anybody telling him. Just as he told me, I had a normal delivery and was discharged from the hospital, embracing my baby. With regard to having children, I thank God that Gerbole has proved to be a real servant and minister of God in following up my case from hopelessness to pregnancy and staying with me, even during my labor, just like a doctor.

Bekako Duguma

I had heard a lot about Prophet Gerbole and had for a long time wanted to meet him in person. One time, when I was sent by the main office of World Vision in Ethiopia to start a development project, we were introduced to each other by phone, and later we met in person. Even though my schedule was really tight, I went and saw him at the home where they stayed when their children went to school in Nekemte. We talked and prayed together. I have seen that this person is much loved by his children and is gentle and blessed. I have also witnessed that the grace of God is reflected not only in him but is also present in his beautiful daughters, through the respect and love they have for people. In general, the following are points that I have observed in the life of the prophet and ones that would set an example for others:

- I have observed that Gerbole is a true man of God and a believer who reflects the Christian life.
- One of the qualities that God shared with man is love, and love is central to the gospel. I thank God for him, because this person reflects the true and godly love that has been revealed to people.
- The other thing I see in Gerbole's glorified life is that he is not attracted by material wealth. He relates all his ministry only to the will of God and not the weight of the "gold" that comes with it.

I would like to present as an example the story I heard once about an invitation for ministry from England that Gerbole received through a brother. He read a Scripture portion to the brother and then sent him off, after telling him that he would not accept the invitation because it was not from the Lord. When we see the realities we live in, we note that he has an honorable stand that could be an example and encouragement to other ministers, with regard to benefits and the will of God or ministry, vis-à-vis walking in righteousness. He has a higher spirit than Balaam, who calculated his income before he moved.

Just as God was with Samuel, and none of the words of his mouth fell to the ground, I have seen both from my own life and the lives of others that the prophet's ministry is similar.

Evangelist Desalegn Terefe

Long before Desalegn Terefe became an evangelist and began to serve the kingdom of God, he was an addict and a sick person, because one of his legs was affected by elephantiasis. A lady called Siyoum Kuma, who worshipped the Lord beginning from the time of the emperor, told him a secret. "My son, do you want to be healed?" she asked.

"Of course, Mother," he answered.

"Then I will tell you what you should do, but do not share the secret with anybody. There is a prayer gathering that happens every night close by at the home of Mr. Makonnen Negewo. A person is ministering there in secret, and you will find him. Go and ask him to pray for you," she told him.

Here is what Evangelist Desalegn said about what followed and his testimony about this servant of God:

I wanted to go right after she told me, but since the minister was there in hiding, and I needed to meet him during the night,

I waited patiently until darkness fell. As soon as it became dark, I went to Mr. Makonnen's house and met Gerbole. He greeted me and just kept silent. Since I was a sick person, I asked him to pray for me. But he said, "I have not been given a message about you. Come tomorrow." I went back home, disappointed, dragging my huge and swollen leg in the dark.

I met him the second evening. "Do you want to know the Lord and believe in Him?" he asked.

I told him that was why I'd come yesterday.

He said, "I kept you waiting until I prayed, because it is the Holy Spirit who determines about healing, not me." Then he gave me water and said, "Drink this, and two things will happen for you. First, your leg will be healed, and second, you will be filled by the Holy Spirit, and He will change and transform your life."

I received the water and drank it. The chewing type of pain stopped, and the wound and swelling disappeared, allowing me to wear shoes again. From that time on, I stayed close to him and became his assistant as he taught and baptized those who came to that house during the night.

He continued to come repeatedly and minister to us in this way, but one time the cadres of the government found out where he was and arrested all of us, including Mr. Makonnen, owner of the house. The following day, while they were escorting us to the police station, Prophet Gerbole separated himself and just walked away. We were amazed that the people escorting us could not see what was happening in front of them while we, the prisoners, saw him clearly. The following day, he brought a big basket (*agelgil*) of food to the police station. Nobody asked or raised any questions about him.

Another time, when we went to a place called Kelela for the work of the gospel, he saw a tree that the local people were worshipping. He prayed and said, "It is only God who should be worshipped. You, the worker of darkness, who has blinded people and separated them from their God, I destroy both you and this tree, and pray that the darkness that is over the people be removed and that they return to God."

The tree dried up, and the heart of the people turned from demonic work to the gospel. God was glorified in Kelela.

Pastor Hambissa Tasisa

I have greatly benefited from knowing Prophet Gerbole closely. I have learned a lot from him about living by faith, relying on God, having patience, loving those who hate us, doing good to those who persecute us and spoil our names, sharing oneself and giving, and listening to God. May the Lord bless him.

Prophet Gerbole is a person whom God raised as His servant in our generation to serve His will. I am privileged to have been able to prove this in many ways.

He never does anything without first hearing from God and understanding His will. He loves to do things after hearing God and knowing His will. He does not want to do anything unless God talks to him. He would not hold back from doing whatever God tells him to do, even if he has to pay a price. I have seen this in his life and ministry many times. Here are some examples:

When invitations for ministry come to him, I have never heard him respond right away that he will come and minister. He may say, "Pray; it will happen if God says so."

I see him saying, "No, God has not spoken to me," even when people try to do all sorts of things to convince him. There were times when people came to me to plead for them when they got negative responses. I would then say to him, "Why do you say no? It would be good if you would go and minister to them."

He flatly would refuse, saying, "God did not speak to me." There are places where he went and ministered at his own expense, without being asked. He is a minister who has decided to serve not by the direction and pressure of people but by the guidance of God. As a result, sometimes his responses are difficult to understand for people who do not know him.

One time we went together to a certain place for ministry. After lunch, we were in our room, talking about the work of the Lord, when a certain sister came in tears, asking the man of God for prayer. I had much compassion for her because of the amount of tears she was shedding. But Gerbole simply watched her. She was well dressed, and judging from her appearance, she seemed to have a good life. She kept on begging repeatedly, "Man of God, please pray for me." Gerbole said to her with a loud and angry voice, "No, I will not pray for you!"

I was shocked as to why he would say that to the lady. But she asked again without being discouraged and in tears, "Man of God, pray for me."

I was even more shocked when he said to her, "What you need is not my prayer but repentance. Therefore, repent and be reconciled with God. How can you sin by doing the things you do?" He started to tell her the things she'd done, as if he was reading from a list. She could not stand and fell flat on the floor and repented. Then I understood that God has remnants in this generation like the New Testament apostles, who did not listen to what people said but exposed those who were lying.

Gerbole does not want only to know the will of God and do it; he also is wise about how he does it. As a result of this, I feel that some people might not fully grasp what God is doing through him. Our people are used to having their eyes closed in prayer when there is a prophetic message or a healing or a miracle happens. But what differentiates Prophet Gerbole from others is that he does whatever God tells him or instructs him—saying a verse, prayer, or taking any action—in the midst of casual talk and fellowship. One time, a certain priest who was a man of God said this to me about Gerbole: "People who do not know him continue to wait for results he has already finished for them." Another person who traveled with him from Addis Ababa to Nekemte in a car said that each statement he made and each action carried a message. In addition, that person said, "Also, God tells him about everything, and everything is true."

One time I heard someone give this testimony: A man had transported a load of coffee to Addis Ababa and after selling it, he was robbed of 72,000 birr. He was confused and did not know what to do. He said to himself, "How can I go home after I am robbed of all this money? What would people say? Shall I take my life? How can I do that as a Christian? What then shall I do?"

While he was struggling with these thoughts and talking to himself in front of the Shoferoch Hotel, someone shook his hand and said, "Peace be to you," in the Oromo language. Following his greeting, the man said, "You were robbed and lost everything you had, right? Why didn't you give to God what was His? This happened to you because of that. By the way, my name is Gerbole."

When the man heard his name, he was happy, because he knew of him as a result of his fame. Continuing on, Gerbole said, "After this, do not take what is God's for yourself. Now, go in and rest. In the early morning, a person will bring some money for you to buy merchandise to take back home. You will not buy less than what you used to buy before. So now go and rest."

The person continues his testimony:

> I used to buy merchandise with the money from the sale of the coffee and return home. I went back to my room and slept very well. As was said, a person I knew came very early in the morning. He brought 10,000 birr for me to purchase merchandise and to pay him back later. I was very happy, and then when I went to my supplier to get the merchandise, he was pleased to see me, as he had heard about the robbery and was sorry. As we talked about what God had done, he said to me, "If there are additional items you need, you can take them and pay me back when they are sold." God fulfilled what he said through his prophet, and I returned home with lots of merchandise.
>
> Since my family had heard what had happened to me, they could not believe their eyes when they saw me. They were all very happy. My father-in-law called me to his house and advised me not

> to worry about what happened and that I could work and gain back what I lost, as I am young. He then promised to give me one truckload of coffee to sell and pay the loan I used to buy the merchandise. Now, everything is back to normal.

The man had actually invited Prophet Gerbole and me to dinner and shared his testimony. God sends messengers, even to those who feel hopeless in Merkato. He saves them from death and changes their stories. But it seems like it would be hard to agree and go to such a place. To those who listen to Him, God will be with them everywhere.

One time, we went to a certain place together for a conference, which lasted three days. On the third day, Prophet Gerbole prayed for sick people in general. He did not give any words of revelation, and the prayer time was very short. After the prayer was concluded and we were transitioning, a certain elderly woman from among the assembly started jumping and pointing to her belly, and shouting, "It is not there! It is not there!" And all the people in the assembly who saw her were jumping and falling. Some were confused and stood up in order to try to properly understand what was going on. We were also confused, because we did not know what was going on. Later, we understood that the lady had had a distended belly like a pregnant woman. Earlier, people who did not know that it was a sickness had made different comments. But I saw God doing a miracle through this short prayer of the prophet, pleasing the assembly and healing this elderly woman. Glory be to God! Since Gerbole does things according to what God wants, one needs to follow closely what he does using the gifts from God. Otherwise, one could easily miss it.

Recently, my wife and I went with Gerbole and his wife to a restaurant for dinner. After we ordered our food, people who were looking for him came, and they ordered their food too. While we were waiting for our food, two ladies came and sat down, and two foreigners followed them and sat with them. Prophet Gerbole focused on this group and stopped talking to us and the group that was looking for him.

The two ladies and two foreigners ordered drinks and were served. But Prophet Gerbole's focus was still on those people. While he raised his hand, suddenly their bottle disintegrated, and the drink was spilled on all four, although I do not know whether it exploded or fell. Embarrassed, they left in a hurry, as if chased by someone. Gerbole then ate his dinner with us.

About his love for all people, he loves all people from the bottom of his heart, without making differences between them. Because of this love, his greetings and approaches are unique. It looks odd to those who do not know him. He has compassion for people because of his love. He is considerate and shares whatever he has with them.

An evangelist said, "One time when I was walking hungry in the city of Nekemte, Prophet Gerbole met me. As soon as he found me, Gerbole said, 'You are starving, right?' even before he greeted me. He then took me into a restaurant and ordered two meals and two soft drinks. When the food came, he said, 'It is all yours. You bless and eat it.' But seeing that the meals were two, I tried to say both of us had to eat. He said, 'You eat well so that you will not be hungry again.' I ate very well and from that day on, the Lord changed many things," the evangelist said. Because of Gerbole's love for people, he shared what he had with this person and helped him to be a source of healing for his generation.

At the end of 2000, I stopped working for the government and started a ministry. The church at that time was going through difficulties. One evening around seven o'clock, I met Prophet Gerbole when I had only one birr in my pocket. He was in a hurry to go somewhere. We met at a taxi stand, as his desire was to take a taxi. He said, "You have a birr, right?" I answered quickly, telling him that I had one birr, thinking that he wanted me to pay his taxi fare for him. He said to me, "What I have is one birr. Bring yours, and let us exchange." I gave him mine and took his. When I looked at it later, it was ten birr. I was surprised. He understood my problem and gave me priority by taking my problem on himself. Because of his love for people, he puts others first instead of himself. God has not let him down because of his actions. God blesses the righteous (Psalms 5:12).

What the Lord Jesus did through Prophet Gerbole cannot all be put on paper, because it is too much. For me, Prophet Gerbole is a very special person. The Lord has done wonders and miracles for me and my family through his support and prayer. I gave this short testimony so that it would be a lesson to others. May the Lord bless you.

Merga Sima, General Secretary of Western Ethiopia Region Evangelical Churches Association

> When the Lord saw her, his heart went out to her and he said, "Don't cry." Then he went up and

> touched the coffin, and those carrying it stood still. He said, "Young man, I say to you, get up!" The dead man sat up and began to talk; and Jesus gave him back to his mother. They were all filled with awe and praised God. "A great prophet has appeared among us," they said. "God has come to help his people" (Luke 7:13–16).

As we saw in the Scripture above, the visitation of God raises the dead from the grave. Our brother Merga Sima, because of God's visitation, returned from the grave. He is also an eyewitness of what happened to two other persons. He gives us his testimony for the glory of God:

A friend of mine, Dereje Dasga, was seriously sick and getting medical attention for some time, but at the end, the doctors said he should go home, because he had no hope. We took him out of the hospital and had to keep him in a hotel room overnight in Nekemte, in order to take him back to our community by bus. That night, I got news that Gerbole was in town. I looked for him and found him. I took him to the hotel where the sick brother was and asked him to pray for him. After the prophet prayed for some time, he said, "This is the work of witchcraft. What is desired is for father and son to die as a sign to you. After a little while, you will hear that the son back home is sick. Since God has intervened, both of them will be healed. This is just as a sign to you."

He then approached the sick person and said, "Since the sickness is in the head, it will come off you like clothing from head to toe." The sickness then began to move down. Gerbole would ask at intervals, "Where do you feel it now?" The patient would reply, "In my chest, in my back, in my knees," and in this way, the sickness came out and disappeared.

Gerbole told the patient to get up from his bed and do some physical exercises, and he did. The person became healthy and whole again. Just after I saw Gerbole off and returned to the hotel, they told me that the son was seriously sick and had been brought to the hospital. We were not perturbed by the news, as the work of witchcraft was already dismantled. The son became well, and we returned home with both of them.

The second person whom God returned from the brink of death is a person called Abdisa Gobena, a colleague in the organization where I work. We were traveling from Gida to Nekemte when he said to me, "Merga, I do not think I will make it this year—I will die."

Even as I tried to calm him down by saying. "You will not die; the Lord is there for you," he kept on uttering more serious things. Even after we reached Nekemte, I stuck with him for fear that he might kill himself with the handgun he had with him. I kept watching him. In the midst of this situation, I met Prophet Gerbole on the street with other people. I told him that I needed him very badly, but he said he was with people and would come to me later. When I told him that I would not let him go, he went with us to the place where we were staying. I asked him to pray for Abdisa. After he looked at Abdisa very intently, he said to him, "Are you at peace?" Abdisa answered, "Yes, I am at peace."

"What kind of peace do you have? You had only a few hours to live, and now they are coming down to minutes. You are not at peace," he told him. He prayed for him and said, "Death, which had come to take you, is gone. Now live!" He is still living, worshipping the Lord.

Pastor Eyasu Tolesa

> It was he who gave some to be apostles, some to be prophets, some to be evangelists, and some to be pastors and teachers, to prepare God's people for works of service so that the body of Christ may be built up until we all reach unity in the faith and in the knowledge of the son of God and become mature, attaining to the whole measure of the fullness of Christ (Ephesians 4:11–13).

The gift of prophecy is one among the gifts God gave for edification of the church. In identifying the distinct features of true prophets and expressing his respect for Prophet Gerbole, Pastor Eyasu has the following to say:

True prophets are:

- faithful to God's Word,
- persons of faith,
- persons of prayer,
- persons of love, and
- humble in character.

Gerbole's faith and prayer are practical. I would like to give as an example what happened in Gambela, when I had the opportunity to minister together with him at a meeting. The month was March, when the temperature is the highest, and it had reached 104 degrees Fahrenheit. People were dying as result of the heat. Gerbole said to me, "I am going to pray that God will send rain to cool down the weather. Do you believe?" I told him I did believe. Together, we prayed a short prayer and went to bed. In the morning, the situation changed so much that it was even difficult to go to church, due to the heavy rain. The weather in the area became cool, and we were able to complete our ministry and return home in peace.

Mrs. Tadelech Degefu, wife of the author
of the Amharic edition.

God has spoken to me and comforted and counseled me through Prophet Gerbole. But a unique case and one in which God intervened directly was during my father's illness. Our father was seriously sick and was brought on horseback from the countryside, supported by people, and received medical care while staying at my sister's house. His sickness was not only an emergency, urgent and scary, but also was always changing. What he complained about during the day was different from that at night. He would be deeply stressed and suffered a lot, especially during the night. One evening, he could not breathe, as if something blocked his throat. My relatives, who were scared about the consequences of not breathing, called me by phone immediately and told me. After we prayed in our house, my husband called Gerbole and told him the situation, giving him the phone number where my father was.

Gerbole prayed by phone for my father, who was not able to breathe or talk. "You who are blocking his breath, release it," he ordered. The thing that blocked my father's throat left him, and he was able to breathe and speak instantly. We were able to call and talk to him in Addis Ababa right away. This was a miraculous visitation of God that happened within my own sight.

CHAPTER 16

CONCLUSION

As we neared the completion of this book, we asked Gerbole, "In your journey of thirty-seven years, from the beginning to the preparation of this book, what counsel would you have for the ministers and leaders of our generation and the church in general?" He began his response by referring to those who were the early examples to him in Hebrews 11:33–38:

> Who through faith conquered kingdoms, administered justice, and gained what was promised; who shut the mouths of lions, quenched the fury of the flames, and escaped the edge of the sword; whose weakness was turned to strength; and who became powerful in battle and routed foreign armies. Women received back their dead, raised to life again. Others were tortured and refused to be released, so that they might gain a better resurrection. Some faced jeers and flogging, while still others were chained and put in prison. They were stoned; they were sawed in two; they were put to death by the sword. They went about

> in sheepskins and goatskins, destitute, persecuted and mistreated—the world was not worthy of them. They wandered in deserts and mountains, and in caves and holes in the ground.

We are the fruit of the tears and labor of those before us who paid a heavy price. From the 1960s to 1980s, there have been many fathers, mothers, and leaders of evangelical churches who cannot be forgotten. They paid a heavy price for the gospel work that began in our country. Here are just a few:

- Pastor Tefera Gonfa
- Pastor Deresse Geleta
- Evangelist Duresa Dinsa
- Evangelist Seketa Geleta
- Mrs. Megerse Shanko
- Mrs. Gole Makonnen
- Mr. Aga Hirpa
- Mr. Dinsa Geleta
- Mr. Debelo Geleta
- Mr. Getachew Muleta
- Mr. Gebula Amente
- Mr. Bekele Guyo
- Mr. Tolera Ereso
- Mr. Gemechu Debelo
- Mr. Nigussie Kuma
- Mr. Abebe Ayana
- Mr. Abetu Ketil
- Mr. Welane Kitil

- Mr. Kitata Gerbi
- Mr. Gerba Teso
- Mr. Makonnen Jergora
- Pastor Tesfaye Haile and his wife, Mrs. Messeret

In Nekemte, Mrs. Shege, and in Gida, Mrs. Lomi Dinsa Sebom, are two mothers who served ministers tirelessly and who sacrificed themselves and their lives to the Lord and the saints. They fed the hungry and gave rest to the weary, hid and comforted those who fled persecution, and sent them off when they moved on. They continued to do this for many years.

Others traveled around for a month or more, visiting believers and encouraging them. When they were persecuted and chased away, they left behind their farms and cattle. Armed vanguards of the community not only put them in prison and chased them away so that they would deny their faith but also forcibly opened their mouths with sticks and poured homemade liqueur down their throats.

Evangelist Seketa Geleta is one of those whose mouth was forcibly opened with sticks and liqueur poured down his throat. He is still serving the Lord. Mrs. Gelane and Mrs. Gale were paraded naked in the market, where people were gathered in the town of Ende. When they were asked, "Will you deny or be paraded naked in public?" their reply was, "We will not deny the Lord. It is an honor for us to be paraded naked for the Lord who was crucified naked for us. But woe to you who would parade us naked."

They were made to walk around naked on a Saturday—a market day. Both the system and the people who made them walk naked are not there anymore, but these sisters are today married and have children and continue to be a blessing to many.

We are therefore the result of the labor of the few we mentioned above and many others. The work of God is not the work of one person but a result of the contributions of many. The house of God is made up of contributors. My standing in the Lord and ministry is a result of their labor. And it is not only my work but the great work of God that was revealed and the growth of the churches that are the result of the tears of believers of that generation. In those days, the prayer concerns were the salvation of people, the outpouring of the Holy Spirit, and the second coming. The return of the Lord was our greatest yearning. When people met, they used to encourage each other by saying, "Do not be afraid; the Lord is coming."

When we compare the spiritual life of that time and today, there was obedience, agreement, and discussing and understanding each other and the fear of the Lord. Today, there is no fear of the Lord. The God who was near then is far now. His glory is no longer among us. Even when people wronged each other, one who sought peace would take himself as the offender and ask for forgiveness. Today, there is boldness; no one would say, "I am the offender." Even when he is at fault, he argues and does not repent or ask for forgiveness. He counts offenses. At that time, a person who grieved by the fall of his brother would cry and intercede, saying, "Lord, remember him; forgive him; return him to his heart."

But today, a person laughs at his brother's fall and spreads the word at great speed. He is not concerned about his brother. We need to understand that God is concerned about the weak. Earlier, people used to look out for each other. Today, people run away from each other, turn away their faces, and pass by. Ministry used to be by the guidance of the Holy Spirit. But now it is by human choice and hence, there is no power. Even though the Word and prayer are key powers, they have been left aside. The Christian of this age who does not understand repentance does not have satisfaction. He who collaborates with the world, forgetting his obligations, disregarding his responsibilities to the Lord and is swallowed by sin must return to his place or else he will be hurt at the end.

May the Lord bless you and give you faith!

Printed in the United States
By Bookmasters